THE RAINBOW BRIDGE

Paul C. Dahm

Running Tide Press
Box 302
Oceanside, OR 97134

TABLE OF CONTENTS

Prayer for the Animals--Albert Schweitzer

Preface   i

Part I   The Rainbow Bridge

Chapter I   Animal ESP, Intelligence, and Empathy   1

Chapter II   Dogs in History   11

Chapter III   Ghosts and Apparitions   19

Chapter IV   English Ghosts   27

Chapter V   My Experiences with Ghosts   33

Chapter VI   The Strange and Unexplainable   43

Chapter VII   The Moment of Dying   49

Chapter VIII   Grief   59

Chapter IX   Saying Goodbye   65

Chapter X   Lasting Memories   73

Chapter XI   Heroes   81

Chapter XII   Hunting--Its Advocates   93

Chapter XIII   Hunting--Its Adversaries   111

Part II   Dogs, Cats and Other Animals in Prose And Poetry

Dogs   125

Cats   135

Other Animals   135

Prayer for the Animals

Hear our prayer, O Lord--for animals that are overworked, underfed, and cruelly treated; for all the wistful creatures in captivity that beat their wings against bars; for any that are hunted or lost or deserted or frightened or hungry; for all that must be put to death--and for those who deal with them, we ask a heart of compassion and gentle hands and kindly words. For all these things we give thanks. For reverence for life is the highest court of appeal.

Albert Schweitzer

PREFACE

In the years preceding the 20th Century, man lived in close proximity to the animals. He depended upon them for food, clothing and their companionship. In 1900, 80% of the U.S. population lived on farms or worked in the food industry.

When the mechanistic age dawned led by Henry Ford's assembly lines, times changed rapidly. A mass exodus began to the city and the "good life" as exemplified by the factories. "Why, Ford is paying $5.00 a day!" was the cry. Like Robert Browning's rats, they followed the Pied Pipers of industry. By the depression, 50% of the country was urbanized which exacerbated the gloom of the early 30's.

When man left farm life, he abandoned a priceless heritage. On the farm the animals were his daily companions, and they added a dimension to life no city could provide. If you have the time, take the opportunity to visit a nearby family farm or visit wih people who raise animals. They share a dimension and vision of life alien to the city dweller.

Animals have fascinated me all my life. Some of my best friends are dogs. Over the years I have searched the literature for references to animals, and this book is the result of my endeavors. I was surprised by the myriad of thoughts and insights I unearthed.

Whe Pope Sirius in 391 A.D. burned the library at Alexandria, which was founded by Ptolemy I in the third century before Christ, all of the accumulated knowledge and history of mankind disappeared in the flames--and all the writing of the earlier era's feelings and thoughts about animals. Only a few thousand volumes were saved and one million volumes destroyed. Had the early Christian church followed the Greek Way rather than the Roman Way, such a sacrilege could have been averted.

I hope these sayings, literature, and poetry will convey to you the love humans have experienced over the years to our friends, the animals. The following thoughts guided me as I wrote this book. Will James said it most succinctly: "To my way of thinking, there is something wrong with a person who doesn't have a soft spot in his heart for an animal of some kind. With most folks the dog stands highest. (The cat has recently surpassed the dog as the favorite pet in the household. *Author*) Then comes the horse; with others it's the cat (*in James' time*). Monkeys are fussed over, but whatever kind of animal a person likes, it's hunky-dory as long as there's a place in their hearts for one or a few of them." (James said these lines in a movie taken from his book, _Smoky the Cow Horse_ in 1929.)

Another Prayer for the Animals

And for these, also, dear Lord, the humble beasts who with us bear the burden and heat of the day and offer their guileless lives for the well-being of their country, we supplicate Thy Great Tenderness of heart for Thou hast promised to save both man and beast, and great is Thy loving kindness, O Master and savior of the world.

Prayer of St. Basic of Caesarea, 370 A.D.

Chief Seattle once said, "If all the beasts were gone, man would die from loneliness of the spirit, for whatever happens to the beast happens to man. All things are connected. Whatever befalls the earth befalls the son of earth."

Lois Flying cloud said, "All animals are expressions of the Great Creator. Would He limit them? Would He only exist in man?"

Cerminera said, "Animals are more closely related to us than we can imagine. Their mental processes are the same: they have fears, feel pain, express love and emotion, become frustrated, and are able to show joy and gratitude."

Mohammed, the Moslem prophet, believed: "The animals are a people like ourselves and shall, when released from earthly pain, share the joys of heaven with man."

Rolling Thunder, a holy man, asks, "How can man understand life if he is not part of it? Man must learn to live in the heart of animals."

Rachel Carson said, "We can never be truly civilized as long as we kill another living thing."

Mad Bear of the Iroquois said, "There are different levels of consciousness with which we have no contact. The unconscious is one. Consciousness is found in animals, plants, and everything in nature. We must learn to recognize these consciousnesses and to honor them."

Do animals live on an equal plane? Consider this example: Some years ago at the University of California, psychologists conducted the following experiment:

Subjects were placed in cubicles and attached to an electrical machine. They were asked questions by another person who administered electrical shocks for each wrong answer. The questioners continued to administer shocks, though they could plainly hear screams and the expressions of pain and agony from the test subjects. A similar test was conducted with monkeys. An outstanding difference with the monkeys was that the wrong answer still resulted in an electrical shock to the subject, but the questioner was rewarded with food. After administering one or two shocks, it was found the monkeys would rather starve themselves than inflict pain on their fellow monkeys.

All suffering is interrelated, whether it be man's or animals' suffering. In our time, Somalia and Yugoslavia have caused endless pain in the world. The acts of man affect all nature and its myriad life forms. When we can learn to be ethical toward all creatures, man will enter into a spiritual relationship with the universe.

Advertisements, such as sending out a fur catalog to all American Express card holders, should be banned. Their logo: "Winter is long and life is short." Animal-rights groups across the world urged card holders to take scissors and cut up their cards.

St. Francis of Assisi wrote: "There is no degradation in the dignity of human nature in claiming kinship with creatures so beautiful, so wonderful, who praise God in the forest as the angels do in heaven." The Sioux believed the buffalo would return to be hunted again. They prayed to the animal's soul, asking his forgiveness, and explained the necessity of the acts. Such an animal rested easily and was thought to be happy he had given his life.

The Kwakiutl Indians of British Columbia believe a dead salmon returns to the salmon country. Great care is taken with their bones which are thrown into the ocean.

The Ottawas in Canada believe dead fishes' souls pass into the bodies of newly emerging fish eggs. The Minnetaree Indians believed the bones of the dead buffalo were once again clothed with flesh and returned the next year to be hunted once more.

The Dakotas buried animal bones as a sign of no disrespect and believed the bones would rise again as another animal.

"Men must learn to listen to the invisible voice, the spirit of the land itself." This was an ancient Indian belief. Louis Flying Cloud said: "If you learn to listen to the wind when it calls and discover the language of the other animals, you cannot lose the center of your being."

Forgive us our trespasses

Little creatures everywhere

James Stephens--<u>The Snare</u>

THE RAINBOW BRIDGE

Far beyond the sky in another dimension lies a beautiful enchanted land. It is the resting place for all the animals who have served man, many of whom sacrificed their lives to save mankind. To enter this land, the animals cross over the Rainbow Bridge. The Bridge was called so by the angels for its profusion of rainbow-like colors which glow and fade in welcome to the new arrivals.

It is a land of lush green meadows, flowing streams, and an endless variety of trees. There are ponds scattered about for the new arrivals to bathe and wash away all traces of their previous existence. They emerge refreshed after their long journey across the Bridge.

There are myriads of flowers, many growing in vines which criss-cross the branches in the trees. The air is fragrant with their sweet perfumes. Bones and catnip rain intermittently from the air above.

In this magic land, all become young again. The old and infirm run about as they did in their youth. The crippled and maimed are made whole again. The days are spent cavorting across the many fields and enjoying the company of the many varieties of animals here. Most happy, if this can be so, are the dogs and otters who are even more playful here than on earth.

There is but one note of sadness here. It is reflected in the eyes of the animals who were pets of humans who loved them while on earth. If one looks deeply into their eyes, this sadness is seen. They miss that unique love, care, and devotion they received from their own special companion. Many had received more love from their owners than their owners had given to their fellow humans.

And then one day, one special, magic day, your own pet looks up. A familiar sound has reached its ears. Its nose begins to twitch, its ears go up, and its tail begins to wag uncontrollably. It stares, then begins to run toward you.

He knows you have come for him. He takes one great leap and once again is in your arms. Your face is kissed and kissed, and kissed again. You look once more into the trusting, loving eyes of your beloved pet. Together you walk across the Rainbow Bridge, never again to be separated.

CHAPTER I

ANIMAL ESP, INTELLIGENCE, AND EMPATHY

A bone given to a dog

is not charity.

A bone shared with a dog when you

Are as hungry as he, that's charity.

Jack London

For the past 50 years, the Chinese have been experimenting with the relationship of animals to the earth. The Japanese, who are known for their earth upheavals, have long kept goldfish bowls to tell them of impending disasters. The goldfish become frantic before an earth upheaval.

The Chinese noted the barking of dogs and their refusal to remain indoors, snakes abandoning their holes, cattle bawling and pawing the earth, horses neighing and running about, seagulls that fly out to sea, and other birds will abandon the area. Often cattle stampede, and the air becomes eerily quiet. All these are forewarning of an impending earthquake.

The Chinese have also noted fiddler crabs by the millions have marched inland before a typhoon strikes land. Also noted has been the disappearance of bears before an earthquake and particularly before volcanic eruptions. The Russians have noted the same behavior patterns.

Historians tell us that before Mount Pelée's eruption in the Caribbean on May 8, 1902, all the animals were restless, snakes and birds and other creatures evacuated the area. The eruption destroyed St. Pierre and killed all of its 30,000 inhabitants save two--a young girl and a prisoner locked away in a fort high above the city.

Using this knowledge, the Chinese have become world leaders in the science of earthquake prediction. They correctly predicted about 755 of these great natural disasters and have saved millions of lives. They hope someday to be 100% accurate as great computers recently have been added to their forecasting arsenal.

Cats have been seen to take refuge in their favorite spots before it rains. Snakes also hide before a rain. During WWII, cats told their owners of approaching raids during the"Blitz" of London, 1940-43. Their owners were the first to take their places in the underground shelters.

Dogs seem to have a special ESP concerning people in physical peril. They have shown up at the last possible moment and guided people to safety, even returned from the dead to do so. There are many recorded cases of this phenomenon.

A report from Oslo, Norway tells of a case of animal intelligence: Nothing could stop Argo, a four-year-old German Shepherd from rescuing his family when fire swept their home, not even a doorknob. Bjorn Vidar Marthinussen, 29, and his stepsons were asleep when their house in the northern town of Rognan caught on fire. Argo, who had never shown a mastery of doorknobs before, managed to open two doors and race upstairs to awaken the sleeping family.

"I woke up just because the dog jumped up on the bed and was barking", Marthinussen said, "Five minutes later we would all have been dead. This dog is incredible! He is a hero!" All escaped before the flames engulfed the house.

And heroes get their rewards--in Argo's case, a big, juicy steak.

In Perth, Australia, this past January a man stopped to aid a female kangaroo which had been hit by a car. She was dead, but inside her pouch lay a half grown joey. To the great surprise of his neighbors the man took the baby kangaroo home with him.

Two weeks later, he was awakened by the frantic thumping of the joey's tail on the floor and found his house in flames. Grabbing the baby kangaroo, he leaped through a glass window to the ground. Seconds later, his bedroom exploded, erupting in flames.

Anyone who has visited the wildlife refuge in Paris, Texas, is familiar with the case of John Gambill. Many years before, he nursed a wounded goose back to health. The next year she returned with her gander and goslings. This went on for many years until today there are more than 3,000 ducks and geese wintering at Paris. When Gambill died in a Paris hospital, hundreds of geese circled around and around the hospital.

A family in California was awakened during a great storm by the frantic tugging of their dog on the bedclothes. They rose to find themselves knee deep in mud and frantically woke their children and fled to the upper floor. A few minutes later a wall of mud hit the house burying the rooms they had just minutes before abandoned. Ironically, their dog came from an animal shelter and was named Last Chance.

After seven years of mental and physical abuse, Helen left her husband and moved out of the home they shared. When her husband returned from work, he found the house abandoned. Helen , nor any of her personal belongings were there. It was as if she had never lived there.

At first her husband, Ralph, said "good riddance". As the days turned into weeks and the weeks into months, he became a miserable, forlorn man. He went to talk with his minister who suggested therapy and told Ralph he was "reaping the bad seed he had sown over the years". He had created great unhappiness in Helen's life (for she, too, had been to see the minister and told him her story).

Gradually, Ralph learned the fault was his. Helen had been a good and faithful wife. He went to Helen's parents and begged them to intercede for him with Helen. He sent flowers to her and called her saying, "I am not the man I once was". Helen's heart was moved and torn by her indecision, she was thinking of giving Ralph another chance. Then one day a strange thing happened. A skunk suddenly appeared at her back door. The skunk scratched at the screen door, asking to be let in. Helen realized if she let the skunk in, she wouldn't be able to live there herself. Then it dawned upon her that the skunk had provided the answer to her larger question, and the skunk turned and waddled away.

Bill lived next door to Mac, his neighbor's dog. Over the years they were inseparable. When Bill was 18, he joined the Marines and was sent to Viet Nam. One day his parents received word that Bill had been killed in action. From that day forward, Mac became disconsolate, refused to eat even his most favorite foods. Two weeks later Mac laid down and died.

In Trelowny, England, a man named Henry kept a large herd of cows. He was uncommonly good to his animals and often visited neighboring farms and made himself known to each and every animal. They seemed to be genuinely happy when he came to visit. His own animals bellowed a greeting to him every morning. As will happen to us all, Henry died unexpectedly one morning. The hearse arrived and Henry's coffin was placed inside and driven down the long lane to the road. A strange sight greeted the driver: along the fence, cows were gathered, hundreds and hundreds of cows. Even the neighbors' cows had joined in with Henry's. The cows tossed their heads, pawed the ground and lamented and mourned in voices never heard before by any of the farmers who were at Henry's house. They were voicing a last goodbye to their friend.

My friend Bill DuPree who milks a large herd of cows went mushroom hunting. They had to give up their quest as Bill's cows followed wherever they went.

There was a horse called Lady Wonder. She could count like TV's Uncle Ed and seemed to converse with her owner. She predicted the Day of Infamy, December 7, 1941, predicted the election of Harry Truman over Dewey, and passed all the tests Dr. Rhine gave her at Duke University in 1948. Lady Wonder is but one of a long list of gifted animals who performed unexplainable acts.

My own Brandy seemed to have a special sense where disadvantaged people were concerned. I sold flowers at Tommy's Park in Portland, Maine. Each day we greeted hundreds of people. Whenever she saw a person in a wheelchair, she would always jump up on one side of the wheelchair to be petted and give kisses. At first I thought nothing of it, but over time she also showed a special care and affection for every person who seemed to be depressed for one reason or another. It was amazing to see them light up, smile, and go away happy. They often came back for another "treatment".

Then there is Missie, whose very birth was a miracle of sorts, occurring days after the rest of her littler. She had extraordinary ESP and could run through a deck of 52 cards, tapping out the number every time. Missie knew people's dates of birth, even their social security numbers. She predicted Goldwater's defeat weeks before the election. She even predicted the day and time of her own death.

"To his dog, every man is a Napoleon,

Hence the popularity of dogs."

Anon

Animal Intelligence

Henry Beston, the naturalist author of Outermost House said, "Dogs are gifted with senses we will never have and are finished and complete creatures, unlike man. They are not brethren, they are not underlings, they are nations caught in the net of time and life, fellow prisoners of the earth's travails".

We know little of animal behavior or their reasoning abilities. Scientists studying with electron microscopes only come in contact with minute parts of the animal and none of his consciousness. We only know animal intelligence is on a very high plain. Watching a tiger or any big cat hunt assures us of this fact. The higher the intelligence of an animal, the less he is guided by instinct.

Animals display intelligence in a myriad of ways. Chimps can reason, learn to talk using sign language. Squirrels and rats easily master the intricacies of the maze when food is their reward. Dogs carry over objects to stand upon, bring their food dishes to their owner, speak with their eyes to let you know their needs and desires.

This intelligence is, unfortunately, a complete mystery to most humans. Only the very few are able to understand and communicate on a Dr. Doolittle plane. We do not know the extent of their thinking, but we see the evidence from the highest animal down to the lowly bats, bees, and ants.

The naturalist, John Burroughs, strongly believed in animal intelligence; and the Indians referred to this intelligence as "deep knowing". Carl Jung described their intelligence "as part of the great collective consciousness man possesses, and here resides a great depository of all memories, thought and knowledge; it is spaceless and timeless".

As mentioned, few can communicate with the animals. Zoo keepers and their help do, animal shelter people, many vets, and others who raise and keep animals may. It is a very special gift. In Brazil, Francisco Duarte, said to be "retarded", communicates with spiders, bees, wasps, poisonous snakes, frogs, alligators, and rats. Many have witnessed these feats, and he has never been bitten.

Fred Kimball has had a unique relationship with animals for more than forty years. He shares a nonverbal exchange with them. He has the ability to communicate with animals who have passed on. His feats are legendary, and thousands are witnesses to them.

In 1903, Dr. E. D. Buckner stated: "Animals are to be considered as creatures that move and act of themselves and have souls like man which informs and directs them".

Buddhism is the only religion which recognizes the equality of all God's kingdoms. It does not recognize any second-class divisions of life.

Jainism, a precursor of Buddhism, believes in the sanctity of all life even the unseen gnats, and ants and spiders. "Who can, with certainty, say otherwise?", asked Dr. Buckner.

The Tibetan Mahatma Letters, which deal with persons of unusual powers, states: "As soon as any conscious or sentient being, whether man, diva or animal, dies, a new being is produced.

Dr. Buckner also stated: "The intelligence of the lower animals is a complete mystery to us. We do not know what they think, nor the extent of their thoughts, but they have more intelligence than we think, and they possess every principle of every faculty which man does". The same arguments for man having a soul apply equally to the animals.

An Example of Pet Wisdom

Montreal, Quebec. A lady painted the bedroom of her daughter, Melinda. Her sister-in-law insisted upon taking Melinda to her house, claiming the strong smell of the paint would make her sick.

"The next morning, our Dalmatian, Carlo, came halfway down the stairs. He was whining and alerting me to the fact that something was wrong. I followed Carlo to the bedroom as he drew my attention to Melinda's empty bed. Even after I told him it was OK, he insisted on guarding the empty bed until she returned home".

Who says this was not an intelligent act?

Dog Language

We should familiarize ourselves with the following: Ears down, tail between legs is a submissive posture. Hair up on back, tail up, is a semi-aggressive, dominant posture. Hair up, tail up, teeth bared and snarling is the most aggressive posture. You should be very wary and not approach such an animal. Tail wagging, body swaying back and forth is a friendly posture, showing he wishes to be your friend.

Licking another dog's ear is a submissive gesture, as is a dog cleaning out an alpha's ears for mites, dirt, etc. A dog licking another dog's body is a submissive role; he is cleaning them off.

Back leg lifted is to leave a higher mark on a tree or wall (some smaller dogs lift their whole backsides to make a higher mark). Urine marks territory (as with wolves) or announces a dog's presence in the area. Back feet scraping dirt is for a greater acknowledgment of their presence. Even females lift their back legs to mark, just like males, and also throw dirt with a scraping motion of their feet. Male dogs often mark other dogs' territory with feces.

A dog lying on its back, feet in the air, tail curled under its body is about the most submissive posture in dogdom, as is one male anally penetrating another or having fellatio performed upon him.

A dog jumping up on you is a domination trip, as is leash pulling; he wants to be boss. The animal should be emphatically discouraged. The owner must be the alpha, the dominant one, as dogs really wish it to be that way. It's part of the ancient pack behavior. A dog not submissive or controlled by its owner is a threat both to the owner and other people. It is just this type of uncontrolled dog who can easily revert to the wild state. He will roam in a pack killing other animals, especially wild creatures, farm animals, and may readily attack a human being. Dogs must be taught their role.

Animal Souls

"The souls of animals are said to be sent to a vast reservoir of souls to become a part of a great group soul. When it comes time for the animal of the same species to be born, souls are taken taken from the reservoir, but no individuality (from their past life) remains." *(Tibetan Book of the Dead)*. I enjoy the thought of my loving Brandy coming back to instruct another human as she did me.

Man has continued to down-play the intelligence of animals. All plants and many animals are sacrificed, without thought, to benefit man. Trees are fast becoming an endangered species. Man, in his egotism, feels animals have nothing to teach us and forgets Yeats' admonition: "Listening is the greatest of all arts to eternity". We have only just begun to study the dolphins, the whales and the higher animals, such as chimps and gorillas. Carl Sagan said, "There must be a Magna Carta, structured to each animal's level of intelligence".

There is a spirit dog who guards a cliff outside of Sidney, Australia. Each time someone attempts to commit suicide off this cliff (as many have and still do) the dog barks and summons people to that person's aid. Many feel he guards the sanctity of human life.

When you lose a family pet and the heartbroken children ask if they will ever see it again, tell them yes (in another place beyond this place). There is an equal chance they will, equal to our chance of seeing relatives who have passed on. We must convey the fact their pet will not come back to them in this world.

Can Dogs Be Empathetic?

Boston, Mass.: Doctors and scientists studying animals say empathy may be a more sophisticated cognitive process than we imagine. Aristotle said: "Love may be thought of as a strong force binding friends, families and couples with the energy of the atoms.

Of all the emotions most akin to gravity, the sensation that keeps the affairs of humanity on track, is empathy. It is the power to recognize the plight of another and to take on that burden as if it were our own.

Empathy allows one to cry during a sad movie or over the death of a character in a soap opera or a play. If you stand on a corner and look lost, someone will empathize with your plight and offer assistance. Without empathy in our world, it would always be Winter.

Scientists are studying the machinery of empathy--what happens when the body and brain of one person connects with another's. Now they are asking, are the non-humans in the world, the animals, capable of experiencing empathy?

The field is rife with dispute and confusion. Some of the researchers argue that a version of empathy developed with the evolution of animals which care for their young over a protracted period of time, thus showing the ability to recognize a need and responding to that need.

"Even the Maiasaurs in Montana elicited this behavior 140 million years ago", says Dr. Jack Horner at Montana State University in Bozeman, Montana. "They hatched their eggs, guarded and cared for the young Maiasaurs", he said. Others disagree. The researchers argue that to experience true empathy it must be an act of great sophistication, requiring that one minds about what has happened. This demands considerable cognitive power.

To empathize is to understand beginnings, middles and ends; and they also say that empathy demands the ability to distinguish self from others, a skill usually judged by seeing if an animal recognizes himself in a mirror.

Using this criterion, the only animals capable of empathy are the chimps, gorillas, orangutans, and possibly dolphins and whales. The evidence is tantalizing for our pets, to think they may be capable of saying, "I feel your pain".

Dr. Martin Hoffman of NY University points out one drawback of empathy is that "we tend to empathize most readily with those who are most similar to us in appearance, social circumstances, behavior, and the like. To a degree, one is empathetic toward one's own group", Hoffman says. "Underneath, he may be very hostile to another group not aligned with him. Empathy encourages group identification, and groups tend to persist in putting themselves against others".

I'll let the scientists fight it out. I only know the few times I get "down", my little Corgi dog hops up on my lap and licks my face. She chases away all the gloom and at that moment one realizes life is beautiful after all. I don't know what they call it, but I call it empathy.

Evolution and Animals

If dogs evolved more, would they be smarter?

Success in evolution means being able to produce grandchildren at a faster rate than other species. Cockroaches are among the most successful creatures on the planet, and it is said that in an atomic war only the cockroaches and some beetles would survive.

Jane Grey, a paleontologist at the University of Oregon says, "Although dogs would never have a human brain, most dogs are bred for color of fur and shape of nose and body, and intelligence comes in where it may.

Being a "smart dog" usually means a dog that does what we want it do to, but what is smart to us may not be smart to a dog. Smartness may simply mean alertness and a willingness to please--a dog skilled at solving human problems (where are my slippers? Fetch). He may be at a total loss when solving dog problems.

CHAPTER II

DOGS IN HISTORY

The more I learn about people, the more I love my dogs.

Prince Ludwig of Bavaria

Philosophy will clip an angel's wings

Keats

Pythagoras, the Greek philosopher, once stopped some men from beating a dog for "its cries were that of an old friend"

Plato believed in the immortality and the eternalness of our souls and that our souls could be reborn in many forms.

Socrates defended the "theory and doctrine in the Phaedor".

Empedocles once observed, "I, too, have been a boy, a girl, a bush, a bird and a scaly fish in the sea." Dogs have caused no end of laws to be compiled, read, and passed. Dogs have brought endless and boundless pleasure to owners of all kinds from people of royalty to those of the poorest of the poor. They have been consort and companion to kings and and have been the subject of much folklore.

To the Royals of England, the dog had a value of one pound, but to a "freeman", only six pence and that of a "cur", four pence. A herd dog going before the herd in the morning and following home at night was worth the "best ox in the herd". In the old Welsh laws, there were four species: the tracker, a greyhound, a cavet hound, and a harrier. There were three kinds of Curs: a shepherd's dog, a house cur, and a mastiff. Should a wife call her husband a cur, she could receive three strokes with a rod the length of the husband's forearm and the thickness of his long finger on any part of her person save her head.

Xenophon (430?-355? B.C.), friend of Socrates and a famous general wrote: "The perfect dog should be big and have a flat, well-knit head. The lower part of the face should be sinewy, and the eyes black, bright and prominent. Hounds so described will be strong, light, well proportioned swift runners, bright-eyed and clean-mouthed."

Aristotle wrote of "courageous animals with deep voices" and of "cowardly dogs with high-pitched voices. Animals with a narrow chin are of even disposition, and an animal with a narrow waist loves to hunt. Large-headed dogs are the most sensitive and have small ears. Those of painted nose are quick to anger, and those with prominent gums are abusive."

Pliny wrote before the destruction of Pompei that dogs were "the most trusting and faithful of all animals to man".

Theodore Gaza, the Greek who was forced to flee to Rome about 1400 A.D., ingratiated himself with Pope Nicholas V by presenting to him a gift, a dog. "The gift I am sending you", he wrote, "is called the dog. It is, in fact, the most precious and valuable possession of mankind. This one animal is responsible for many and all kinds of benefits to us and is adorned with the highest points of excellence."

Conrad Gesner's _Natural History_ was published in 1551 and contains the remarkable tale of a mastiff bitch who whelped nineteen pups at one birth and at her next birth, eighteen, and at the third, thirteen. "She was", he adds, "black and of a large size".

In Homer's day (1000 B.C.) Many dogs were kept as pets which, according to Blondus, "bark very readily, and their only occupation was the devouring of food". Homer called them "table dogs" since they were only interested in tables already laid and wandered about in search of a free meal.

In China, the Heavenly Dog, or T'ien Ken, is a power of considerable antiquity; and in one of Peking's main streets a temple is dedicated to the god, Erh Lang, the destroyer of dragons and protector of dogs. It is he who owns the dog which is heard howling in the sky and occasionally eats up the sun (eclipse). The appearance of a comet and the noise of thunder have been considered to be the celestial dog on his way down from heaven to the earth.

Animal Traits

Wouldn't humans be more gentle and loving if they had the gentleness of the rabbit and lamb, could work like a beaver, have the courage of a lion, the cunning of a fox, and tiger, and the fortitude and resilience of the wily coyote (whom man is hunting to extinction)?

Shouldn't our families be like those of the wolf, whose members care for one another with sincere love and devotion? We need the common sense of the horse, the strength of the ox, and we desperately need the humor, comedy and simple playfulness of the sea otter and the squirrels who dance above us in the trees.

We need to be like those masters of good grooming, the cats, and have the skill to master a job that a dog has. We must learn to express the joy of life which the bird expresses in his song to greet the morning, for it is a new day filled with promise and hope. We must learn to let go of the past. "The birds have complete trust in the One Above and Nature, and this we need most of all", say the ancients.

Another Dr. Doolittle

Kate Solliste

When Kate Solliste was three years old, she heard plants and animals talk. She talked about everything with her kitten, Dusty. Dusty told her animals loved humans, but she didn't understand why she could hear Dusty and others couldn't. Dusty told her they could, but they have forgotten how. She also told Kate not to tell her parents about her talks with animals.

When Kate started school, Dusty told her to begin to integrate the difficult world of human beings. Kate reluctantly agreed. One night when Kate was six, Dusty crawled into her bed and told her she loved her very much. The next morning Kate's mother saw Dusty's body lying beside the road. Kate was inconsolable and began to "shut down" her communication with animals.

It was only in the past few years that Kate has healed her painful past and has resumed her communication with the animals. She can once again hear plants and animals and can help others to learn to communicate with them. This is how she does it:

Kate visited a Labrador who was covered with tumors. The veterinarian said there were too many to operate upon. Kate asked the dog what was going on. The Lab replied that when he was a puppy, the other pups were cared for and he was not. "I felt neglected and unloved", he told her. When Kate told her client this fact, the woman was mortified. "I always loved him the best! The other two were being groomed for show and were to be sold. Getting dogs ready for show and sale takes so much time and attention, but I always loved him and beg his forgiveness."

When Kate told the Lab this, his energy shifted, he forgave his owner, and within two weeks there wasn't a sign of a tumor. "Just like humans", Kate said, "our pets have problems relating to their place in the family. These problems can affect their health."

Kate feels dogs are the conveyors of "unconditional love". They even let us know when it is their time to leave us, when their mission here is done. They will usually stop eating and communicate their leaving to their guardian. It is some consolation for us to know that pets have an easier time leaving this earth than we do.

We, as pet owners, can do much to re-establish the broken sacred bond by treating our pets and all animals we come in contact reverently.

Kibbles and Psychics

Aloha, Hawaii: Bandit was oblivious to everything but his master tickling his ears. B. J. Schmeltzer began to coax him into conversation. Without so much as raising an eyebrow, Bandit, the Lhasa Apso, told Schmeltzer "that he considered himself a lucky dog. He had no complaints; his life was good". "It was good to hear", she said, "because animals don't always tell happy tales".

For example, Winston, a man-sized cross between a Great Dane and German shepherd, recently told her, "My previous owners mistreated me and I ended up at the dog pound". He was very grateful that he had been rescued and thought his new home was the greatest place in the world.

Yes, Schmeltzer talks to animals! Everything from pet poodles to spotted owls. She is one of a growing number of people who call themselves animal psychics and help owners to know what's on their pets' minds. She feels interest in psychics "is only natural, given the huge number of pets and people's fascination with the paranormal. People are more aware now that there are other forces around us--UFO's, ghosts, angels, that sort of thing. People want to know more". Animal psychics have clients all over the U. S. About 40-45% of households own a pet, according to the Vet Medical Association.

Schmeltzer's business, called Animal Communications, get 20-25 calls a week from owners about a lost pet or being baffled by their pet's behavior. Still others are just curious about what their pets have to say. One lady was upset because her Doberman was lifting his leg on the furniture. Schmeltzer told her the dog had heard her talking about moving, and he was afraid to be left behind like his previous owner had done to him.

Schmeltzer's daughter, Carrie, 18, helps her to run the business. They have a toll-free phone, 1-800-730-7255, and they make house calls for $50 an hour. They also do consultations on the phone. "Being a psychic requires a thick skin and a sense of humor", Schmeltzer says, "We get some pretty strange looks".

Judi Olmstead is a believer. She called Schmeltzer to come over and talk to her dog. When she arrived, the dog began talking about Judi's poodle which had died 14 years before. Judi was dumbfounded. Schmeltzer looked at Judi's feet and told her, "Your poodle is still with you". She could see her lying across Judi's feet, much to Judi's astonishment.

Schmeltzer first became aware of her psychic ability after Carrie was born. She discovered a telepathic bond with her daughter, and each knew what the other was thinking.

She has telepathic conversations with animals through mental images or pictures and is often amazed at what she "hears". She tells of a conversation with a spotted owl in the woods. The owl, which had a sense of humor, told her, "he didn't give a hoot where he lived, as long as he had a place to live. He couldn't understand why people were cutting down trees because they create the air all of us breathe". "He told me our modern technology could create the materials we need: Grow hemp, which is non-hallucinogenic marijuana which contains pure wood fiber. It also has many medicinal qualities." Schmeltzer and many others were amazed to learn this. Always we should show respect, kindness, and tenderness toward every living creature. Chief Seattle said it well: "We must treat the animals as our brothers".

Animal ESP

In a recent letter a reader stated: "When two dogs are raised together, there is a bond formed of which we humans know very little. Rex and Rocky are an example: "When Rex became ill with crippling arthritis, we had to take him to the vets to be euthanized. Rocky positioned himself in front of the door and refused to budge until Rex returned. Telling Rocky didn't do any good, and we tried to fill the void by giving him extra treats."

KUD, Orleans, MA wrote: "This is about the Rex and Rocky letter. We also have two dogs. When Spirit was hospitalized, her brother, Silver, searched all over the house for her. He whined and refused to eat. Finally Spirit had to be put to sleep. We brought her body home and laid it at Silver's feet. Silver put his paw across Spirit's shoulder, sniffed the body, stayed for a while, walked away and never looked for her again. He knew she wasn't coming back".

Animals handle death better than humans. It is much more cruel when the animal has no idea of what has happened to a companion who has simply "disappeared". They interpret it as "abandonment" and go right on grieving.

Cambridge VT: "When our horse had to be put to sleep, we removed the halter and brought it back to show his pasture mate. She smelled the halter and ran to a far corner of the pasture where she stood with her head down, grieving. Had we handled it differently, I'm certain she would have pined for a long time".

Panama City, FL: "The best way to communicate to Rocky that Rex is dead is to let him see and smell his body after he has been euthanized. His reaction will be the same as ours. He will nudge Rex and try to wake him up. After awhile he may try to drag the body off and try to bury it. If you don't allow him to do this, he will mourn for a long time".

South Bend, IN: "When you know your pet will have to be put to sleep and he has a pal, let the dog sleep on a pillow so his scent will get on it. After he goes, his will find comfort sleeping on the pillow".

Rochester, NY: We had two cats and two dogs. When our eighteen-year-old cat, Ben, had to be put to sleep, Schatzie, our dog, took it harder than the remaining cat. When our dog, Lady, died, the cat mourned along with the remaining dog. Animals know more and feel more than we think".

Chicago, IL: "I hope you have room for one more story in your book about pets", a lady wrote. "Many years ago a neighbor's dog had pups. I took two brothers. The pups shared their lives--what one did, the other was sure to follow.

They played with our cats, but they respected them . After a few years, one of the dogs was accidentally poisoned and died. I buried him in the back yard and didn't realize his brother, Walter, was watching. Each day for about three weeks, Walter would go and lie on top of his brother's grave.

Years later, Walter became so ill he could barely crawl. I came home from work one day to find that Walter had gotten out of the house, down the back steps and across the yard to his brother's grave. There he laid down and died. He had never forgotten.

I was teary eyed as I buried him beside his brother. Humans could learn a lot by watching what the creatures tell us. There is an old Irish saying: 'The creatures were placed here for us to take care of them, and they to care for us". (Virginia, Anadarko, OK)

CHAPTER III

GHOSTS AND APPARITIONS

Somewhere there is a little dog of mine,

Somewhere a little dog does wait,

It may be at a garden gate

With yelps of glad delight

To welcome me home at night.

Anonymous

Can pets return from the dead? Consider the following stories:

Earline Wahl told me that soon after her pet dog, Lady, died, she felt her presence near her on successive days. One morning she was tending her horses when she heard Lady's bark. Looking up she saw Lady outside the front stall, the home of Lady's favorite horse. As Earline ran toward her, Lady vanished. The same thing happened the following week and the week thereafter. She has never seen Lady since.

We both felt Lady, with whom Earline had been inseparable, had come back to tell her and her friend she was all right and not to worry or grieve for her. I know, because Kristen did the same thing for me two weeks to the moment she died.

Before I was given Kristen to care for, she had lived like a gypsy on the boundary of an alien world, a world deaf to her entreaties for love and affection. She never was able to overcome her distrust of strangers, so deeply had she been abused. It was the night of a full moon, and I was awakened suddenly by a movement at the foot of the bed where Kris always slept. I felt something brush my leg and could physically feel I was not alone and that she was there with me. I couldn't see her, only a shadow. I could only feel her presence. Earline and I both feel that, as with her experience with Lady, it was Kristen's way of saying she was okay now and happier than she had been in this world. She was at peace, and it lessened my sense of loss.

It may sound strange, but such occurrences are not all that unusual. Many wives tell of seeing and talking to their dead husbands. Where there is a deep bond between the pet and its owner, the pet may return. I know of two other incidents in Maine where this happened. Take Corky, for example:

Corky had been rescued from certain death by his owner. She found him in the woods where he had been shot and was near death. She rushed him to her vet who saved Corky with an emergency operation. She and her husband cared for Corky for seven years until he died. Two years later they moved to an apartment in New York City.

One night she was awakened by Corky barking. She sat straight up in bed: "It wasn't possible. Corky was dead but I heard his bark in the living room." She rose, opened the bedroom door and found the apartment filled with smoke. She quickly awakened her husband and together they roused the other tenants who fled into the cold night.

Later, standing in the street watching the building in flames, she asked her husband, "How could this be?" He shrugged. "Maybe Corky was just repaying you for saving his life", he said. It's as good an explanation as any.

Many spiritualists believe animals are closely tied to some type of group soul. After their deaths they linger here until they are ready to return to that soul. Pets may return to perform a certain task. One lady spoke of walking alone to the hospital to visit her sick husband. She was accosted by two strange men when suddenly a huge black dog appeared barking and snapping at the men. They fled in panic. This same dog appeared every night for the next two weeks and walked her to the hospital. One the night her husband was released, the dog disappeared, and she never saw him again.

In the '70s, at the Breakwater Hotel in Kennebunkport, Maine, guests heard a dog bark and a child cry in an upper room which was vacant at the time. Both have been heard before and are considered to be ghosts.

A dog named Bobby was devoted to the boy next door. Soon after the boy was drafted and sent to Viet Nam, Bobby died and was buried in the dahlia patch in the back of the house. When the boy returned he was delighted to see Bobby run from the dahlia patch and bound into his arms. Bobby jumped up and down and licked his friend's face. Then he bounded into the dahlia patch and disappeared.

When he told his neighbors later that day of Bobby's greeting, they were astounded and disbelieving of his story. Haltingly, they told him that Bobby had died shortly after he was shipped overseas, a year and a half previously.

Take the strange case of a man who was driving home during a monsoon rainstorm in the mountains of Colorado. Suddenly a dog appeared in his headlights, and he was barely able to stop. The dog stood there, and then he started up a rise and then returned. He seemed to be saying, "follow me". The man got out of his car and, as he drew closer to the dog, it seemed to be his old dog, Jeff. He knew this couldn't be true. Jeff had died the year before, but it did look like Jeff and, perplexed, he walked closer to him. He followed the dog, keeping him in the flashlight beam. As he reached the top, an astounding sight greeted him. The whole road was blocked by an enormous landslide. He looked around for "Jeff" but he was nowhere to be seen. If he had driven over the rise, his car would have gone off the road and into the canyon 2500 feet below. "Jeff" or whatever it was, had saved his life.

Carlos Castenada, speaking to Don Juan, says: "Man must understand the spirit of the animal. It is not merely a dog, cat, a horse or a wolf, it is a spirit like we are".

Ichabod Crane was not the only one to see the ghost of a horse. Spectral horses have been heard for hundreds of years, galloping down nameless lanes, always heard but never seen. They are so real people jump out of the way at the sound of galloping hoofs, but no horse appears.

The only proofs man has of immortality are the many ghosts who inhabit houses and fields all over the world. Ghosts have haunted houses for hundreds of years and appear and disappear at will.

A Summer visit to Yuma, Arizona is best avoided. The temperature often reaches 110° and higher. The area is intersected by canals as water is more precious than emeralds in this vast desert.

There are three ghost legends worth noting. One is a poltergeist who refuses to allow any dwellers in his house. Many have tried but have given up as he empties kitchen cabinets, drawers in dressers, and bangs and clangs pans all night long.

Sadder still are the ghosts of women crying and calling out to their lost children who have fallen into the canal and drowned. A spectral dog has been heard barking mournfully. Another lady, known as Llonia, helps parents to keep their children from the fate of her own offspring. Parents tell the children if they venture too near the canal, Llonia will steal them away and they will never see them again.

The beautiful and mournful Daphne is another more vivid ghostly legend. The day before she arrived from the East in 1932 to rejoin her husband, he was thrown from his horse and was killed. Lost in her grief, she did not see her two children fall into the canal and drown. Unable to control her sadness, Daphne hung herself from a rafter in her husband's rented hacienda.

In ghost lore, many who kill themselves have commited an unpardonable sin and are condemned to haunt the earth for all eternity. Many tell of hearing Daphne calling out to her children on misty, foggy fall nights. A dog is heard barking and a child's voice is heard calling out for help.

The hacienda is deserted now. Legend says Daphne haunts the room of her death, and she has been heard softly crying through the closed doors. The caretaker's cats refuse to enter the room and often run away, their hair standing on end.

A medical doctor named Williamson once treated a stray dog who had severely sprained his foreleg. Over the next five years after this dog's death, it appeared at the good doctor's house, scratching on the door for admittance. This happened each time he was with another dog with a "leg problem". As Doctor Williamson began to treat the injured dog, the other simply disappeared.

All these ghost stories point out a single moral. If some stray chances into your path who is cold and hungry, possibly injured, take them to your heart and hearth immediately. They may be the only treasure you will find in this life, no matter how long you may live and how hard you may search.

Many believe pets return to help their former owners. I believe this and often call upon Kristen to help me overcome my yelling at careless drivers. She hasn't cured me yet, but each time I do, I think of her and renew my vow to stop.

Too many animals have returned for us not to believe they survive death. It is most comforting for me to think I'll see Brandy and Kristen again across the Rainbow Bridge. The Indians believe all forms of life are sacred to the One Above and He considers each equally. The Indians say if one does not respect all life, including all of its forms, one can injure one's own spiritual development and will never become a whole person."

Socrates and Aristotle and Plato all believed in the immortality of all life, and Jesus preached this philosophy. The ancient Egyptians mummified their animals as well as their pharaohs, and many cats have been found perfectly preserved.

Gandhi said, "The greatness of a nation can be judged by the way it treats its animals". William Blake stated: "Each man is haunted until his humanity is awakened". In this sense, ancient Egypt was a great civilization.

More Ghosts and the Supernatural

Dunninger

Dunninger was a famous mystic and mind reader who gained world-wide fame for his feats of legerdemain in the early 20th Century. When he was questioned about his conjuring tricks, he replied: "To those who believe, no explanation is needed. To those who do not believe, no explanation is possible."

"Miracles"

The psychophysical anomalies we call miracles point to an afterlife. When Joseph of Copertino levitates, or Padre Pio produces the stigmata, or Theresa Neumann stops eating and drinking (as well as eliminating) for 35 years, we are watching material existence being transmuted into forms that closely resemble a spiritual afterlife.

Near-Death Experiences

A little girl lost consciousness and was taken to the hospital. On the table her heart stopped. The doctors applied electrical shock therapy to restart her heart. She was gone for almost three minutes before a shock re-started her heart.

Shortly afterward she regained consciousness and returned to the bright little girl she had been. When she was questioned and asked if she had been afraid, she replied: "No I was not. My brother and his dog were with me and he looked after me." What the little girl did not know was that she did have a brother, but he had died a year before she was born. She described him exactly as he had been remembered by her mother.

Carl Jung (1865-1961) renowned Swiss psychotherapist, after a near-fatal heart attack in 1945 told these stories: As he lay in bed, "I had a vision of a delegation protesting my death". He said of his experience, "Death is a sense of such completeness that once we are inside of it we will never wish to return". He also related the story of meeting his dead father during this illness. His father gave him a most surprised look and asked, "What are you doing here? You're not supposed to be here yet."

Those who have had an NDE (Near-Death Experience) become more appreciative of life, love other people more, are less materialistic, less concerned with pleasing others and more concerned about the meaning of life. They now enjoy an overwhelming increase in self-confidence, security, and self-esteem. These changes are lasting as they are more positive, and they no longer fear death even though:

"Death is the undiscovered country from whose bourn no traveler returns."

Dreams and Reincarnation

Abraham Lincoln had a dream wherein he was dead. People were gathered around his bier and many women were weeping and wailing. He was elected president shortly after this dream.

Prince Michael of Greece, who has written a book called _Living with Ghosts,_ reminds us that Abraham Lincoln is said to haunt the White House, "and he has been seen by many people." He also indicates that dogs and children are particularly sensitive to ghosts

A friend tells me of an experience she had in a rented house built in 1920. After she turned the back bedroom into an office, her Shih-Tzu, Chew Shu, kept going into the closet and facing the corner would bark incessantly until she put him out of the room. This happened so many times that she mentioned it to her neighbor, who had lived there all her life. The woman's eyes grew big and she stammered, "But that's the closet where the original owner hung himself!"

General George Patton regularly held conversations with his long-dead father who appeared to him. Patton claimed he had fought with Alexander the Great and with Caesar in Gaul. He claimed to have lived many lives before this, and his position in life was to lead great armies in battle. He was killed in an auto accident in 1946 and may be waiting to return once more.

All goes onward and outward

Nothing collapses

And to die is different from

What anyone supposes

And luckier

Walt Whitman

Strange, is it not? That of the myriad who

Before us pass'd the door of Darkness through,

Not one returned to tell us of the Road

Which to discover, we must travel too.

The Rub'aiy'at

Corbin says, "All the soul's powers are assembled and concentrated in the sole faculty of active imagination". At death, then, we are released into the imagination and what we see is the soul's image, and this is the light of which the NDE speaks.

The imagination is everything.....this is where we came from, this is where we are going."

Terrence McKenna

"We do not know and do not understand the evolutionary implications of such things as mediumistic transports, near-death visions, out-of-body travels, anomalous time perceptions, apparitions, poltergeists, miracles of saints and avatars, and a good deal more. Such things and phenomena may be only the beginning of a vast evolution of the species mind."

Michael Grosso

26

CHAPTER IV

ENGLISH GHOSTS

In some Canine Paradise

Your wrath, I know, rebukes the moon

Sir John Lucas--The Curate Thinks

The folklore of England bristles with legends and tales of animal ghosts and strange phenomena. A whole book would not cover these happenings. Here are a few for you to consider:

A primary distinction: If the ghost appears in front they are still alive. If they appear behind you, they are dead.

In old Ropley, there is a cottage haunted by a cat. A former tenant met the cat on several occasions. It would appear and then disappear quite suddenly.

The tenant believed it to be her mother's ghost as the cat walked in the same manner as her mother.

Workmen working on a former art center said they were troubled by the ghost of a large black cat. The new owner dismissed their fears as "nonsense".

She soon changed her mind when she, too, saw the cat. It was the size of a dog and all the doors were locked at that moment. The foreman related the room became suddenly ice-cold and the locked door opened. As he closed it, it opened again and a monstrous black cat with flaming red and orange eyes was crouching outside. The men fled in terror.

A shadowy figure was also seen which stated in a deep bass voice, "You cannot see me, and you even don't know who I am."

The new owner, a Mrs. O'Brien, had an exorcism performed and all was quiet for a year. Some actors staying at the center performed a seance which seems to have once again opened the doors for the cat's re-appearance.

Tom Corbett, a famous psychic, believes his animals are more in tune with psychic vibrations than we humans. His boxer, Biddy, has backed away, hackles raised, as she entered supposedly haunted houses and rooms. Corbett says animals have the same right to haunt places as men and women do. Many psychics agree with him.

Barbara Cartland, the author, had trouble with a ghost dog at her house. It was the same home where Beatrice Potter had written *The Tale of Peter Rabbit.* Candles were often snuffed out as if by an invisible hand. Cartland had the house blessed by a priest. "It saves a lot of trouble with ghosts", she said.

She also told the story of her dog, Jimmy, who had to be "put down". Soon afterward her other two dogs acted very strangely at mealtime as if they were afraid. They growled when nothing was there. Her Murray was particularly disturbed and would back away from his food. Soon afterward Jimmy began appearing around the house. Cartland called in a noted psychic, but he found nothing. He did tell Cartland to warn her son he was in danger. She did so, and days later, his manservant ran Glen's car into a ditch, but neither of them was hurt. Jimmy continues to appear every now and then, but Cartland finds it comforting as she was very devoted to him.

The Royal Theatre in Bath has a butterfly ghost who appears whenever the Butterfly ballet is performed at Christmas time. The dancers are attired as tortoiseshell butterflies. As the ballet is performed, a live tortoiseshell butterfly appears and flies around the packed house. Legend says that at every Christmas pantomime the butterfly appears.

Mrs. Joy Battersly, whose setter, Red, who died in 1965 and left the family sorely grieving, has sworn she and the family heard Red barking where they buried him. She was so alarmed she had her husband dig up Red a week later. Until they got another dog five weeks later, Red could be heard barking. Then he stopped and hasn't been heard since.

In Walberswich, near Southfield on the English coast, a white dog which seems to be waiting patiently for its master, has been seen for the past 150 years. A horse rider, Penelope Fitzgerald, tells of being thrown from her horse when he shied at the appearance of the white dog. "It was like a large pointer", and she related. Penelope thought "something was not quite right" when the dog suddenly disappeared in the bracken. She then realized she had seen a ghost.

In the late 1800's, Thomas Davidson kicked a cat which barred his way and saw his foot pass right through it. It reappeared shortly hopping like a rabbit and frightened Davidson half to death.

Apparently, not learning his lesson, he kicked it again, and it grew luminous and his son said Davidson had been paralyzed by the incident and was not "quite right" for some time.

Near this same mill in Newcastle a Mr. Wedgewood reported seeing a tabby cat in the furnace room. It impressed him by wriggling like a snake and passed through the solid stone wall. The mill has become the stuff of legend as donkeys, cats, dog and monkey apparitions have been reported as having been seen in or nearby the mill.

.Many pet owners in England believe an afterlife exists for their pets. Their conclusions are based on their own observations. Telepathy, haunts, and apparitions are possessed by certain animals, but human ESP is more complex. There is no earthly reason to believe animals cannot pass through the portals of death and survive just as we humans expect to do.

In Sussex, a little girl and her minister father saw the ghost of a young girl accompanied by a West Highland terrier. They were seen often and accepted by the new curate as a part of the house. Often a lady appeared to accompany them.

A few years later, the curate's wife decided to remodel the parsonage. During the repairs to the staircase, the bodies of a lady, a young girl, and a Westie were found behind the wall. They were given a Christian burial and have not reappeared since.

Another strange tale was told by Rosemary Brown around the turn of the century. While sitting one day, she felt a heavy weight lying upon her lap. She sensed purring and could smell what seemed to be a tiger which soon appeared to her but not to her husband sitting next to her.

He asked her to describe the tiger which she did. He then told her it must be Sabrina, a tiger cub his family had owned when he was a lad. They had shared their home in Cairo, Egypt when his father had been posted there. Sabrina made many visits to the family before taking her leave.

Mrs. Brown must be termed a psychic for later she saw cobra snakes in spirit forms, a brown bear who was very friendly and stood in her bedroom doorway. She blew in the bear's face (as Barbara Woodhouse suggests we do) and he cheerfully turned and ambled away.

The English use this test for a haunted house: They take a dog or a cat there and if either shows fear, it proves the house is haunted. In many recorded cases, dogs have fled in terror, hair standing on end or fleeing to a closet or hiding under a couch. Cats, however, are less affected.

A certain Grace MacMahon and her brother were taking a walk when they chanced upon an unexpected Georgian mansion and a girl with an Alsatian dog rapidly approaching them down a long driveway. Then they disappeared quite normally over a hill. Later they discovered the mansion did not exist and no trace of it whatsoever has ever been found. Houses appearing and disappearing are not that all uncommon. Two fishermen two years later, reported a similar case in the same area.

The Brishame Black Dog haunts a house where the owner buried a treasure previous to his death and returns at times to guard it. If annoyed, he attacks with strange, unearthly cries and has the curious and uncanny habits of the specter.

Tetcott is inhabited by a pack of hounds as the result of a rash declaration made by one Arscott of Tetcott. Part that he would follow the hunt until doomsday. He was taken at his word, for at night the local folk often hear his horn in the park and the sounds of the pack as it races by in a whirl and a whistle of the wind.

At Okehampton and Tavistock, a gaunt bloodhound runs ahead of "my Lady's" coach and four. Attracted by her charms, men enter the coach and are never seen again. A similar story is that of Dando, the wicked priest of St Germain, and his dogs, who lure his penitents to an evil end.

At Deane Prior, the Black Hound's Pool is haunted by the ghost of a weaver who, after death, returned to his loom and because of this was changed into a black dog by the parson in a simple method of throwing churchyard dirt into his spectral face. The reverend gentleman then led him to a pool where he was given a nut shell with a hole in it and told when he had emptied the pool he might return to his loom. So, very often at midnight, the black hound can be heard bailing out the water which can be heard drifting back through the hole in the shell.

At Sinmouth, an unpleasantly familiar specter exists. This is the Black dog of Salcombe Ridge, who accompanies lonely travelers to Sentry's Corner on dark nights, whether they desire his company or not.

Nathaniel Hawthorne believed survival after death was a reward for surviving the travail of life.

A photo taken at a pet cemetery showed her dead dog, according to Anne E. Bloehin and was shown in a book she wrote, called _That Dog of Yours_, published in 1941. Her pet had run away from a kennel and had been run over by a train. This she learned later on. She then saw her pet running away from the tracks.

In a book written in 1924, _Experiences in Spiritualism_, the Earl of Dunraven reported the story of D. D. Home, a famous medium of the 19th Century, while in a trance stated that animals did exist in the afterlife and that base creatures, such as bees, etc., or wild animals ("base" people, too, such as the "Great Unwashed") were nearer the physical earth, and more advanced animals, such as the dog and the horse, occupied a "higher sphere". He also reported that animals who lived on earth long ago existed in the afterlife.

Metempsychosis (the transmigration of lives and souls) for animals is real. Some horses have astral bodies, as stated in _Life on the Twentieth Plane_ by Sampson Law.

In the book _Trails of Truth_ by Jenny O. Pincock, a spirit is said to have stated in a seance that "it was a crime for little boys to shoot squirrels and so to send their little spirits out of their bodies prematurely".

Pearl Judd, a noted medium, reported "bright, beautiful birds are found in the after-world", and many other noted sensitives concurred.

Peine C., a subject of Pierre-Emile Carnillier, was asked if animals had astral projections. She replied that they did and remarked a light is to be seen around dogs and horses, but it is quite different from the one seen around humans. Another medium, Gladys Leonard, reported in an astral projection, she found herself in a "dark, gloomy yard, packed with domestic animals which were dead, yet alive. These pathetic creatures had just been slaughtered."

Mrs. Eileen Garrett reported in her book of seeing "a gray, smoke-like substance spiral up from dying birds, much like the same 'smoke' rising above a child that has died". The smoke was said to represent the astral bodies of the dying birds.

Mary Bagot was staying at an exclusive hotel. As she sat in the lobby, she saw her pet dog, Judy, run through the area by the desk. She was startled. Judy had been left at home and no dogs were allowed at the hotel. A few days later she received a letter telling her Judy had died the same day she saw her run through the hotel lobby.

Mary Demler was totally devoted to her dog, Mac, and he to her. As she lay in the maternity ward bed after the birth of her first child, she heard Mac walk into her room and lay his nose in the palm of her hand. She was startled to see Mac was soaking wet and dripping water on the floor. Mac made a grunting, characteristic whine and then disappeared.

Later that day, she was told Mac had fallen into a rain-swollen stream and drowned. It happened at the same time Mac had appeared to her.

The National Opinion Research Council conducted a survey on contact with the deceased in 1984. The results were 67% of those with departed spouses reported contact with them, 41% of the general public made similar claims.

CHAPTER V

MY EXPERIENCES WITH GHOSTS

What female heart can gods despise?

What cat's adverse to fish?

Thomas Gray--1775

When I was in the army, we were shipped to Korea where we spent 22 days quarantined in Inchon harbor. There had been an outbreak of nasopharyngitis on our ship, and the doctors declared us contagious. I survived the 22 days without getting sick, being what the army doctors had termed "a good physical specimen".

When we debarked, we were taken to an old factory in Yung Dung Po where heat vents in the concrete floors attempted to warm us. We would remain there awaiting assignment to our units. I promptly became ill and was taken to the hospital in Seoul.

My case was diagnosed as pharyngitis, and I was placed on sulfa and other drugs. At the end of ten days and when my fever had not abated, the doctors ordered another series of x-rays which showed double lobar pneumonia, a serious infection of both lungs.

My fever was 105.2 when the doctor put me on antibiotics, the new "miracle drug", penicillin. I was given the first of one million units which would continue every three hours. The next afternoon I lapsed into a coma as the drugs needed time to fight the massive infections.

That night at eleven, I became a spectator in my hospital room. From above , I saw two nurses bending over me, feeling my forehead and showing great concern for my condition. The nurses were changing shifts, and the nurse who had been on duty was relaying the events of the past ten hours to the night nurse coming on duty. I will never forget her last words: "The next few hours are critical. Keep him in your sight at all times. Call the ward doctor if there is any change".

I realized what she was saying--that I might die in the next hour or two. I certainly didn't feel I was going to die and reached out my hand to both of the nurses. I wanted them "not to worry". I had no intention of dying. Hell, I was only 18 and hadn't yet begun to live.

The nurses gradually faded from my sight, and the next thing I remember was a beautiful angel leaning over my bed. (I thought about calling Heaven to check if they were missing any.) The night nurse joined her and, as I awakened, I saw tears in their eyes. They grasped hands saying, "He's made it."

I wanted to laugh with joy. I was very touched by their concern. I remained in the hospital for three more weeks recuperating. I had been one sick young soldier. The two nurses became my friends, and I had a lot of fun calling them my two guardian angels sent from Heaven above to look after me. To this day I have never forgotten them even after more than 40 years. I had, what they call today an "out-of-body experience".

It was not my only foray into the paranormal. In the early 1970's I was living in Kennebunkport, Maine. There were ten places which I found to be inhabited by ghosts. One of them, the Breakwater Inn, had three different sets of strange happenings.

One was a baby's cry and the sound of a woman weeping and a dog barking. The older residents told me a maid at the Inn had a child "out of wedlock" and, unable to live with her shame, killed the baby and herself. Often when guests lounge on the deck talking and drinking, an eerie silence descends over the revelers. "Shhh! Don't you hear her?" "Listen to the baby's cry." Many on the deck feel they hear a woman sobbing and the muted sounds of a baby's cry. Many are frightened out of their wits and hurriedly depart. The appearance of these ghosts is accented as the moon nears its full phase. Strangely, there are no reports of the cries during the winter when the Inn is mostly deserted. The ghosts (apparently) need an audience before they will announce their presence. Many reservations near that room have been canceled. Those guests who have stayed near the room have left without looking back.

The Breakwater also boasts a beautiful lady who appears in the early morning hours carrying a cat in her arms. Those who have seen her say she has "long, black hair, is dressed in a flowing diaphanous, black lacy gown. She "passes" through the locked door and seems to float across the floor. As she nears the desk, she asks the clerk if they have a room". (It is most unusual for a spirit to talk.)

The strangest part of her appearance is that she is seen after the Inn has been locked up for the night. All the windows and doors are barred to any entrance. She seems to appear out of nowhere and depart in the same manner. No one in the town knows anything about her, who she is, or where she came from. The most popular guess is that she has come to meet her lover who will arrive the next day, but he never comes.

Her sudden appearance so early in the morning has caused many desk clerks to be seized by terror. A few have been nonplussed, grasped by confusion and have stood trembling, unable to move or speak. A few have tried to question her, never getting an answer. One young man ran screaming into the night as she entered, and was never seen again. He never returned to pick up his pay check. To this day she is an enigma, an unsolvable mystery, but she is very real to those who have seen her.

The other ghosts are a dog who barks and a man whose footsteps are heard in the hall but is never seen. Some conjecture it is the lover of the lady in black, walking the halls looking for her room. The dog is thought to have accidentally been left behind and is barking to be let out of its room.

More eerie and more frightening is the Captain Lord mansion which was refurbished in 1971-72. The new owner had enticed some recent college graduates to help him. They lived rent free and were promised financial rewards from the enterprise when the mansion re-opened. (None of these promises was ever kept.) Like many Maine seacoast mansions, it had been built in the early 19th Century by Captain Lord, a successful sea captain. He was married to a most beautiful woman who was as evil as she was beautiful. She treated the help with disdain, was discourteous to townspeople, and was well known for her disagreeable disposition. As the years passed, like Dorian Gray, she became more wicked in manner and action. Her death in 1858 was not a cause for mourning in Kennebunkport.

Not too many years later, the people who lived in the mansion (the Captain died in 1862) reported they had seen Mrs. Lord and heard her slamming doors in the upstairs rooms. As her legend grew, the mansion had a succession of owners until it fell into disrepair during WWII. It remained so until the present Greek owner bought the place in 1971.

I had lived in Cape Porpoise at this time, a few miles away, but spent much of my free time at the mansion, being caught up in a series of

36

happenings. I had developed a romantic interest in Margaret--a water-color artist who was one of the residents. Margaret was enamored by sunsets, for which Maine is famous. Her imagination took full flight here, and her paintings of sunsets were spectacular. Our whole group became sunset devotees, and each evening we gathered at the Breakwater Lounge to watch nature's wondrous displays.

Alas, my romance with Margaret was doomed from the start. The more I learned about her, the less my passion for her. Margaret, like many artists, was totally self-involved. She cared little for the group and they, in turn, cared little for her. Each went his or her own way.

Strange things began to happen at the mansion. At night we heard sounds of someone moving about upstairs though we knew we were all downstairs. We heard doors slam and objects being dropped on the floor. The strangest happenings took place in Margaret's room. On bitterly cold nights her locked windows would be opened, and she would wake up freezing.

She would return to her room and find her belongings scattered about--tubes of paint missing, along with personal objects, such as jewelry. All these events had a deliquescent effect upon Margaret's fragile emotional state. Her manner, and her eyes especially, took on a haunted look. She began to talk to her deceased husband who had committed suicide. She begged his forgiveness, blaming herself for his death. Often we found her crying in a corner, staring out the window. She needed help which we were unable to give her.

One morning we found Margaret had suddenly disappeared during the night. All traces of her were missing from her room--paintings, clothes, personal effects--all that we associated with Margaret. She never told anyone she was leaving, and I was very sad for she had not said goodbye. I had been her champion, and I would miss our walks and rides seeking out the beauties of Maine, especially the rainbows in the wind-driven snow after a NorEaster. None of us ever heard from her again. It was as if she had never been a part of our lives.

As the months passed, I began to understand Mrs. Lord's poltergeist behavior. Mrs. Lord seemed doomed to inhabit the mansion for all eternity. Was this to be a punishment for her past life? Was Margaret headed in the same direction? It was very evident to me they shared much in common. She may have been a Jacob Marley trying to warn Margaret to change her ways. Or would Margaret be like Marley and Mrs. Lord--doomed?

I learned of other haunted houses and places in the Kennebunkport area, ten in all. More were found if you went down the coast to the Maud Muller fountain. It no longer exists, but it was a favorite stopping place for admirers of Whittier's poems. The man who owned the property had constructed the fountain as a tribute to the judge in the poem and his lost love, Maud Muller. Legend tells of Maud and the judge walking hand in hand and they have been seen sitting by the fountain. The new owner felt the visitors a nuisance and destroyed the fountain in the mid-1970s. Where do the judge and Maud roam today? Were they a conjecture of ratiocination?

There was an old mill west of the Port, said to be haunted by two men. They had been killed in a grisly, unsolved murder in the 1890s. The mill has a still, forlorn air about it, as if haunted by a foreboding presence. Though I walked in the area many times, I never found a trace of haunting though people in the area swore it was true. The men had killed one another over a woman, it was said. One surprised the other two, killed them, and then committed suicide, a common enough occurrence in our soap-opera days.

There is a building in what was once a church on the campgrounds leading into Old Orchard Beach. I became friends with the owner's daughter, Alicia, and she told me of many strange happenings to summer visitors who rented the building, now turned into a small lodge. She remembers booking reservations which specifically excluded the lodge. The story Alicia told me was the minister had slain his mistress with a sword which he then placed on top of the church's pulpit. The pulpit and sword are said to mysteriously re-appear and once again run red with the blood of the slain woman.

It is well known by the family that a poltergeist inhabits the lodge and harasses the unsuspecting tourists. A friend of mine, Brian, rented the lodge one winter, and his window was opened on below-zero nights and his clothing and belongings mysteriously disappeared, I told him about Margaret's experiences at the Lord mansion. He laughed at me. He was secure in his warm bed of egotism which protects the smug and arrogant, assuring them their lives are above reproach. Two months later, Brian disappeared from Old Orchard Beach. Whether he left out of fear or a need for change of scene, I do not know. I often wonder about him, if he is still so complacent.

Other tales of ghosts drifted by my ears like the soft fogs of Maine's early June. My favorite is the ghost of a man at St. Anne's Episcopal Church in Kennebunkport. This is the same church ex-president Bush and his wife, Barbara, attend when they are in their summer residence at Walker's Point.

I have spent many nights there. The church is on a large spit of land right on the ocean. Mists and fogs steal in with great regularity turning the trees and bushes into ghostly apparitions from which cascades of dew cling and fall. Often a tree appears, as they did in the <u>Wizard of Oz</u>, reaching out to ensnare one as he or she walks by.

The story is this: On one of those foggy nights in the early 1930s, a man hanged himself from a tree in the churchyard. Popular conjecture has him a victim of a thwarted romance. Still other stories tell of bankruptcy, theft, and the stock market crash of '29. Chose whichever best suits your outlook on life.

All we know for certain is that he appears on foggy nights, a great coat drawn up around his face. Some have heard him wail like some banshee, others have heard him sob. More rare is coming across his body still hanging from its rope in the tree.

I never missed a foggy night, often with a new love, Marjorie, who found it great fun. A couple of times we hid in the bushes as the stabbing lights of flashlights held by the church guardians who searched for us. We laughed with delight at our ease in evading them, but we never did see the hanged man.

I feel he, too, is doomed to haunt the churchyard. Suicide, as Dante tells us in the <u>*Divine Comedia,*</u> is the great unforgivable sin. To take away the reality and the beauty which life grants us is unpardonable. The hanged man has been seen, head down, almost totally enshrouded by fog; he has been seen walking, trailing a rope behind him; and he has been seen hanging from the branch of a tree like in the documentary and song, <u>Strange Fruit</u>. Those who have seen his face swear it is twisted and distorted by pain.

My last personal experience with ghosts is the most harrowing. During my interest in the history of Mrs. Lord, I spent a great deal of time studying her portrait in the parlor near the front door. Try as I might, I could not peer into her spirit. I waited for her to turn into Dorian Gray, but she did not.

Summer turned into the brilliant hues of fall. No other place on earth can match a New England autumn. The colors must be seen to be believed. Each vista and tree becomes a new aesthetic experience. Before I knew it, October 31st was at hand--All Hallows Eve--when the ghosts of the departed rise from their graves for their yearly night of life.

Many observers of Mrs. Lord's portrait swear she was alive and stared back at them. I decided to test the veracity of their reports. At 11:55 p.m. on October 31, I was poised in the foyer outside the portrait room.

The house was deathly still, the only sounds, my hammering pulse and heartbeat drumming in my ears. I felt goose bumps rise and fall on my body. What if the portrait was really alive? What if Mrs. Lord could will herself back from the dead? All signs told us she was a ghost. What would I do if she appeared before me? My heart really pounded at the question, and I felt my composure slip away.

It was two minutes to midnight when I moved toward the room, hesitating outside the door. My legs refused to go any farther. I had to use all the force of my will to enter the room; and there she was, staring at me.

Was it my imagination or did I see her eyes move? Wasn't her head more to the left the last time I was here? There could be no other explanation--the head had moved, and I saw a glint of light in her eyes. It was unmistakable! It was midnight and Mrs. Lord's portrait had come to life, or so it seemed.

I gasped for breath, my legs trembled and my knees were wobbly. I had to get out of there, but I was transfixed, glued on the spot by those terrible eyes boring a hole in me. I wanted to scream and run like the poor desk clerk at the Breakwater Inn.

At that moment it seemed to me Mrs. Lord was making a movement out of the portrait--so vivid was my rampant imagination. It was the strength I needed to turn and run. I ran to the door, opened it and fled into the foggy mist, expecting at any moment to be grasped by some ghoul from the "Night of the Living Dead".

I ran until I could run no more, all the way to the Booth Tarkington docking shed where I stood, trembling, my chest wracked with pain as I gasped for breath. The fog began to roll in, creating a deeper world of mystery and terror. I ran to my car, revved it up and wasn't at peace until I was home in bed.

What had I experienced? I only know it was something far greater than my comprehension. I had always believed in ghosts, and now Mrs. Lord had proved that belief was not misplaced. I went back to the portrait room one week later and found no signs of All Hallows Eve. Mrs. Lord had returned to whence she came, that shadowy land beyond our ken. Had I not gone back she would have held me in her power. Now I was free of her. It is amazing for me to know she is with us 150 years after her death.

Spurred on by ghost tales on the internet, I made a visit to Baker City, Oregon. A former luxury hotel was being renovated and was found to be inhabited by ghosts. The Geiser Grand Hotel, once Eastern Oregon's most prestigious, fell into disrepair and became a brothel, a veteran's home, and a place for sporting gentlemen before closing in 1969.

The following ghosts have made their appearances: A hotel cook and his assistant were unnerved when a box floated before them in the food closet. A worker who scoffed at ghosts quit and fled the premises when he shared the elevator with no less than a dozen ghosts. He didn't stay to collect his $1000 bonus for readying the hotel for the tourist season.

Two guests on the third floor complained about a noisy party in the room above. When they and the manager investigated, they found an empty room.

The new owner, Barbara Sidway, figures the ghostly activity is inspired by the hotel's violent past. A whole lot of living went on in this place", she said. This included Baker County's first murder trial as the result of a shooting at the hotel.

Most of the ghosts are poltergeists throwing things around and generally scaring the occupants when they appear. Among the notewowrthy is a Lady in Blue, attired in a 1930's dress and veil (similar to the Kennebunkport ghost lady). Another resembles a 1920's flapper.

Both have been seen more than 20 times. More than 25 ghosts have been seen. There is a headless chef who, legend says, was decapitated by the dumb waiter.

By most accounts the ghostly happenings take place long after dark. Tina, the bartender, claims to have been locked in the liquor room no less than 11 times. Another bartender, Tim, admires the ghosts' style and laughs when he sees a beer tap opened.

For those of you who scoff at all this, book a room at the Geiser Hotel and check it out for yourself. I believe--and you will, too.

CHAPTER VI

THE STRANGE AND UNEXPLAINABLE

Fleas are, like the remainder of the universe, a divine mystery.

Anatole France

In the 2500 B.C. "The Instruction of King Merii-ha-re", the whole of human life is viewed in a compressed period of time. A council of deities judge the lives of the newly deceased, deities who regard a human life as if it had been only an hour.

When we ascend to this higher world, we will comprehend the meaning of our lives in relation to the Cosmos, to time and eternity, to God and immortality, and to other unfathomable mysteries. Perhaps we see "through a glass darkly" and then face to face. Now we know in part, but then we shall know as I am known.

Dr. W. Dewi Rees, a Welsh psychiatrist, in his studies involving the interviewing of widows in Japan, found contact with the deceased was common in both men and women. He found the same to be true when 293 widows were interviewed (during the first six months of the bereavement process). Even contact with the spouses 20 years dead were common. Rees believed these experiences were psychological in nature.

In *English Ghost Legends,* we read of the tale of the night watchman who was surprised in the cellar by a man accompanied by a large, black dog. The stranger suddenly struck the watchman who struck him back. The watchman's hand passed through the man who emitted a ghastly shriek as the dog fastened its teeth on the watchman's leg. Both retreated to the coal house which had no other exit. The watchman followed, but he found no trace of either. Since nothing living could have escaped, the watchman concluded it was obvious to him that both were ghosts.

Camille Flammarion tells of being given a room belonging to a man who had just died. He was awakened by a noisy disturbance in the kitchen. The noise continued for an hour or more.

When silence returned, he saw an animal of unknown origin dart up the stairs and jump out a window. He was amazed to find the window covered by an impenetrable screen of wire and iron. He could find no trace of the noises heard in the kitchen area. Nothing was broken or disturbed. The same manifestations were repeated for three days when Camille's mother stayed in the same room.

In *Survival After Death* (1920), Charles L. Tweedale told the tale of a haunting where his dead Aunt Leah was seen repeatedly. Her apparition was accompanied by the ghostly forms of her recently departed Cairn terrier. It is a famous case of animal and master being re-united in the hereafter.

In *The Authentic History of the Bell Witch*, M. V. Ingram tells of "door scratchings and other noises which grew progressively louder and moved from upstairs room to room. It was soon determined a "witch" was present in the house who taunted the residents, pulling their hair, slipping their warm covers off the bed and other hauntings. The "witch" supposedly appeared in the form of a dog-like creature which disappeared when fired upon. Eventually John Bell, the father of Betsy Bell who was the focal point of the haunting, died mysteriously, and the "witch" was blamed for his death.

Nandor Fodor, a medium, "psychoanalyzed" the "witch" who said she was at one time the spirit of an unknown buried near the Bell home. Ingram added "this intruding force was perfectly aware of the concept of human survival and of haunting spirits".

The Drummer of Tedworth is a poltergeist haunting of many grotesque effects. On one occasion scratching noises were heard within a bed. After witnesses searched the bed, the weird noises ceased but were replaced by the panting and cries of an invisible dog. These circumstances have never been clearly explained.

Witchcraft and Satanic Lore

The appearance of supernatural animals has always been part of witchcraft and satanic activities, according to Raymond Bayless. In his book, *Animal Ghosts*, Bayless contends a black poodle appeared to Faust, and similar beings "are related to the demonic dogs and other creatures which supposedly bedeviled the saints, an all too unreliable group of witnesses".

"Interestingly", Bayless adds, "animals were kept by witches and played the part of familiars. In certain cases, these pets were fed on the witch's blood; and this vampire practice prevailed so that a supernatural bond was created between the master and her pets."

For centuries, cats have been associated with witchcraft, much more so than dogs. This relationship has been explored intensively and the belief is still held in some areas that witches could easily change into cats. With this idea came the concepts of the werewolf and were-animals in general

The annals of witchcraft are filled with tales of animal familiars (dogs, cats, horses, tigers, etc.) And this rich lore suggests that a possible foundation of fact may be found in these lurid myths and legends. It may be similar to the origin of the ideas about ghosts.

In the case of phantoms, it was for years claimed that from the dreams of the dead sprang the concept of ghosts and, in turn, religions. It is not true, for the idea of ghosts began with ghosts which are very real. Ask anyone who has seen one.

The combination of the mysterious and apparently devilish violence of the poltergeist led our unsophisticated Puritan forefathers to believe in the concepts of witchcraft. Egged on by the misguided and unbalanced Cotton Mather, many women came to horrible ends, burned and hung, the victims of superstitious thought.

These events were not capable of being explained by the Puritan's leaders. The primitive psychology of the times led to the excesses. The animal familiar, the apparition was misinterpreted. This led to the hellish 1670-1695 interventions, the burning of witches. The animal, especially the cat, became the traditional familiar of witchcraft.

Can Animals Astrally Project?

One Mrs. Beauchamp awoke during the night to hear her little dog, Megatherium, running into her bedroom. Her husband also heard the dog's pawsteps and said it was their pet. They arose, searched the room but found no Megatherium. In fact, they noticed their door was shut. Mrs. Beauchamp felt their dog had died, but in spite of her alarm, fell back into sleep.

A short time later, she heard her daughter knock on her door and cry out their pet was dying. The family dashed upstairs and found Megatherium almost strangled by a strap wound around his neck. The strap was removed and Megatherium recovered completely. The family had no explanation for this strange incident

A strange apparition consisting of a wagon drawn by horses (no driver) was heard as well as seen on a number of occasions.

There are many forms of psychism which do not conform to any rule and remain curios and sometimes bizarre anomalies.

Psychics tell us: "If humans can pass through the wrench of the Portals of Death, there is absolutely no reason to deny animals this gift. All evidence points to this fact: animals do survive death and, on occasion, are capable of manifesting their continued existence through 'apparitional' and 'haunting' phenomena."

In other word passage of myths, fairy tales and legends, and in the fantasies of the otherworld, there lies a land which is found just beyond the Rainbow Bridge. It is believed by many that at the moment of death one's whole life flashes before them. Pooh-poohed by many, newly revealed near-death experiences have shown this to be true.

In the _Tibetan Book of the Dead,_ the Lord of Death is said to observe the life of the newly deceased in the terms of their relationships with other people and with the kingdom of animals. He who has been kind and gentle and loved by his creatures is rewarded with an eternal association with them. The _Book of the Dead_ tells us we must "first learn how to die, and then thou shalt learn to live." It is a fact that our society ignores, and turns away from death at every turn. We are so afraid of death we have convinced ourselves there is nothing afterward.

Socrates told us, "Then beyond question the soul is immortal and imperishable and will truly exist in another world." And Plato, "Our soul is immortal and never at all perisheth."

In automatic writing, Suzanne Smith tells us of Helda Gibbs who wrote from the beyond: "At the moment of death there was no pain. I wasn't unhappy or happy, frightened or lonely for I saw my father, my sisters and my brother. They weren't asleep but quite close to me.

"My message to the world is that death was the happiest moment of my earth-life. Of course, it was much longer than a moment, but the wonderful freedom from pain, the feeling of peace and security when I saw my beloved dead alive, smiling, waiting for me, drove away loneliness, fear, and for a while, all the grief of separation from my two boys (still alive)....I do want people to know whatever they are afraid of, they need not fear death. It is the beginning, not the end of the road."

People on their death beds hallucinate. Healthy people hallucinate about the living, but terminal patients hallucinate about the dead, and religious hallucinations are very common, such as an angel or a saint coming to take them by the hand. Scott Rogo said, "A dying person might easily misconstrue a white, apparitional form as an angel of mercy." Many dying people are elated at their moment of death, and 83.1% saw close relatives by their side.

Mac and Old Pete

Mac was the most treasured possession of Pete and his old woman. They went places and did everything together. One day they were out hunting and Mac took out in pursuit of a 'coon. He soon left Pete far behind, who followed his baying voice.

As Pete came over a rise, sudden silence met his ears. He ran ahead and came upon a deep pond in the stream. He quickly surmised Mac had followed the 'coon into the water.

Pete jumped in after him. A short time later, they found themselves on a narrow winding road which they followed until they came to a gate across the road. It was guarded by a smiling young man who greeted Pete warmly, saying, "We've been expecting you." Old Pete was overjoyed to be expected by anyone.

The young man went on about the glorious land which lay beyond the gate and the house which had been prepared for him. Pete hung on his every word and called Mac to follow him through the gate.

"Hold on there", commanded the gate guard, "We don't allow any dogs in here." Pete thought for a moment and then said, "I don't want to go into any place which doesn't allow dogs." He called to Mac, turned and walked away with the young man calling after him to come back.

Further on down the road they came upon another man dressed in a flowing white robe. "Welcome, Old Pete. We have been waiting for you. My name is Michael."

Old Pete's eyes glistened and he said, "Me and Mac are dead, right?"

"That's true, and dogs are welcome here in Heaven, Pete. Down the road they can't let them come in for they would soon smell the fire and smoke and brimstone and warn their masters. Come right in, Old Pete, everyone is waiting for you."

CHAPTER VII

THE MOMENT OF DYING

In dreams I see him spring to greet

With rapture more than tail can tell,

Their master of the silent feet

Who whistles o'er the asphodel,

And through the dim Elysian bounds

Leads all his cry of little hounds.

John Halsham--My Last Terrier

Eleanor Holmes rose up in bed, her sister holding her hot hands.

"'Natalie', she said, 'there are so many of them. There's Uncle Fred--and Ruth, what's she doing here? Oh, I know.' (Ruth had died the week before. Chill after chill went down Natalie's spine.) "Her voice was so surprisingly clear." 'It's so confusing. So many of them!' "Suddenly her arms went up into the air, as when she had welcomed me. 'I'm going up', she said. Immediately afterward, Eleanor was dead."

DeWitt Miller, in a 1942 Coronet article said, "In view of the stubbornly ineradicable faith that the cumulative evidence indicates that the moment of death is often a time of glad reunion, I have come to the conclusion, it is."

Elaine Worrel told of a strange experience she had in Anaheim, California in 1969. She was living in a boarding house at the time and had a nodding acquaintance with one of the other roomers, Patricia Burns.

She was getting out of the shower on the day when she smelled the distinct odor of strong pipe tobacco. Slipping into her robe, she went into the hallway where she was met by a tall, young man smoking a pipe and carrying a Persian cat. He motioned her to follow him and then paused at Patricia Burns' room. Elaine pushed open the door and nearly fainted, for Patricia was lying on the bed covered with blood. She had slit her wrists. Elaine quickly called a doctor.

Later when Burns was recovering, she thanked Elaine for saving her life. She explained: "I had been drinking and thought I should rejoin my dead husband." She then showed Elaine a picture of her husband holding their Persian cat. It was the young man who had directed her toward Patricia's room.

The Grandmother Who Said Goodbye

On the night of January 10, 1979, the Reverend Mr. Tweedle was awakened to see an image appear on the panels of his wardrobe. Indistinct at first, it became clearer until he recognized his grandmother. Her face was as perfectly distinct as it was in life. Then it gradually faded away.

The next morning he relayed his strange visions to his parents, only to see his father rise from his seat and hurry from the room. His mother told him his father had awakened to find his mother standing by their bed. When he rose to speak to her, she faded away.

Later that morning they received a telegram announcing the grandmother's death during the night. They later learned his father's sister had also seen her mother's apparition at the foot of her bed holding a long-deceased pet.

Guardian Angels

A TV show has sparked a growing awareness in guardian angels. The Catholic Church teaches that we are each allotted one at birth whose job is to keep us free from harm and sin during our lives. They have long been in the literature. Husbands and mothers are very good at it, also. They often come back to guide and give advice to their beloved.

One dead father appeared to his son, Gary, when he became separated from his hunting companions. It began to snow, and he was very frightened, as he was only 14. He looked up to see his father standing by a tree and he said, "Don't worry, son, follow me." They walked along and the son noticed his father left no footprints. After an hour or so, they came across his companions who were looking for him. He looked around, but his father had vanished.

It was some time before he could tell his mother what had happened. She, of course, understood. She feels her husband's presence often, but she has never seen him as Gary has.

Psychics

Most of us have some psychic ability and occasionally experience deja vu. Some have an ability to read people's hands, interpret Tarot cards, and sense what is happening in other people's lives.

Sherry Dresser's mother in Kennebunkport, Maine, could hold a person's hand and in 20 minutes discern who that person was and what was happening in their lives at that given moment. It was awesome to behold as she was always right. She could have been a professional medium if she so chose; and I was afraid to let her read my palm.

Psychic mediums are chosen by the dead to act as communicators between them and their loved ones. One lady was contacted through a medium two years after her husband's sudden death which had left the family destitute. Then, through the medium, he told her of three insurance policies he had hidden in a cubbyhole. She retrieved them and the family from that moment on had no more financial worries.

Still another man advised his wife to be wary of a man trying to buy an interest in their business, now run by the wife. He contacted her through a mutual friend with whom he had been very close. The friend wrote to the dead man's widow. A few days later, he received a call from her telling him the night before she, too, had been contacted by her dead husband. He stood by her bed, and she heard him say, "Kick that man out!" She told him she had no reason to believe the man wasn't the "right sort" until "your letter and his appearance caused me to doubt him". She had been seriously considering his offer.

She contacted a private investigator to look into this man's background. He turned out to be a confidence man who had committed bigamy and deserted both wives. Any relationship with him would have ended in disaster for her and her business.

Animals may share this gift. Many dogs have died hours after their beloved masters' deaths and, in one recorded case, a canary named Petie fell off his perch, dead, an hour after his mistress died. In one famous Civil War case, one Captain Peters was severely wounded and taken back home. His faithful dog lay at his side during the days he struggled to recover from his wounds. "Alas," the chronicler writes, "gangrene set in and the captain soon died. His dog, at the moment of the captain's death, left, went out on the porch, lay down and died."

Many psychics are used by the police to help in various murder cases where they have no clues. These psychics are able to visit the murder scene and reconstruct the murder as it took place. Often they are able to furnish police with accurate descriptions of the murderer or to find clues which lead to their apprehension. They do not always score perfect accuracy, but their records are remarkable. One psychic was arrested for the murder of a woman whose body she saw in a vision. The police surmised only the murderer could know all these facts. Later events showed the psychic not to be involved.

Our first American medium, Mrs. Lenore Piper, was investigated by the psychologist, William James, in his forays into the supernatural relating psychology to psychic research. He found her powers to be without explanation.

The Pilgrim's Vision

"The weary pilgrim slumbers

His resting place unknown

His hands were crossed, his lids were closed,

The dust was o'er him strewn

The drifting sod, the mouldering leaf

Along the sod were blown,

His mound has melted into earth

His memory lives alone

Oliver Wendall Holmes

Aldous Huxley, the author of <u>Brave New World</u>, was well known for his interest in the psychic realm. In 1965, two years before he died, he gave instructions to Keith Reinhardt about certain books in his library he wished his wife, Laura, to read. In one, the third shelf from the floor, the sixth book on the left, she found a book in Spanish.

As instructed, she turned to page 17 and counted to line 23. There she read: "Aldous Huxley does not surprise us in this admirable communication in which paradox and erudition in the poetic sense and the sense of humor are interlaced in such an efficacious form. Perhaps the majority of listeners to this conversation will not have an idea of the spiritual richness of this communication through the summary which the faithful translator and learned scholar in scientific disciplines, who is Alicia Jurado, has made for us."

Another gifted psychic, Irene Hughes, also gave a book test to Rev. Paul Higgins. He writes: "Mrs. Hughes had never been in our house and knew nothing of my library. She said she felt the presence of William Butler Yeats and that he wanted me to read a poem he had written about a priest which he felt fitted me. I would find it on page 87 of a little red-covered book in my library.

I jotted down this date but was unimpressed, knowing I did not have a book of Yeats' poetry.

"Upon returning home, however, I went through my shelves of poetry, suddenly coming upon a little red anthology in which there were three poems by Yeats. I found the one referring to the priest on page 187, not on page 87. It was a most flattering poem and raised my spirits high. He outlined the travails of my ministry very well. I granted the right to Yeats to be incorrect about the page number."

Beyond the Pale

Bill and Judy Guggenheim have presented an interesting premise. It is their contention that we can communicate with our deceased loved ones. "Ask for a sign", they say, "that they still exist."

Your question may not be answered immediately. For one lady, it took three months before she received her sign. The key is to ask. There are two things important in the life of a grieving person--patience and determination to take care of oneself on the road back to happiness and health", said Clark Morphew, the religion writer for the St. Paul Pioneer Press.

Several months after Deborah's brother died, she was awakened by someone shaking her leg. When she opened her eyes, she saw Joseph, her brother, sitting on the edge of her bed. "He looked real", she said, "just like you or I sitting there, and he looked vibrant--alive. He radiated a warm, yellowish-white light, like an aura.

"He hugged me, and I felt his hug--warm, wonderful and loving. I could even smell the cologne he always wore."

Joseph told his sister everything in his world was fine and told her "not to worry".

"We were able to communicate telepathetically", she said. Then the light began to fade, and Joseph disappeared.

In a related story, my friend, Tina, said, "I was in the kitchen and all of a sudden my cat Raymond's hair stood on end, and she was hissing. Then our dog came out of the living room barking and growling, his back up". When Tina looked up, she saw her brother sitting in the family rocking chair. "He was smiling, and then he just faded away. I knew he was OK at that moment, and my grief began to pass", she related.

Many of us cannot rely on these miraculous voices and visions. Miracles happen in surprising ways when you don't expect them, but they happen when you need them most.

Meditation is a good way to deal with your grief while awaiting a sign. Daily play soft music, close your eyes, and empty yourself of expectation. Gradually your pain will fade away. I do, and it has brought me even closer to my beloved Brandy and the no-longer-appearing Kristen.

I am not the only one who feels our pets will go to heaven. In Rotterdam, Holland, theologian Werner Stamm says, "All our pets go to heaven, even hamsters and rabbits, and it's the same heaven for all of us." The famed religious leader says he has interviewed over 300 people who have survived near-death experiences, "and they have shown me all animals go to heaven."

Dogs, for example, are mentioned over and over again in the Bible. St. Francis always blessed all the animals and was often seen preaching to the birds. Many of those Stamm interviewed told of seeing their beloved pets once more. As a result, they are leading lives free from the fear of death.

Shadow

Carl Segran of Texas says when he almost died during an operation, he was re-united in heaven with Shadow, a gentle horse he had loved as a boy. "I saw myself surrounded by rolling fields that seemed to stretch for miles", (just like the land beyond the Rainbow Bridge). "Shadow, the mare I had raised from birth, was standing waiting for me. She was prancing and tossing her head like a young filly. I grabbed her mane and pulled myself up on her back. Off we went, over the hills we rode so long ago. Then, just as suddenly it ended, and I was in a hospital bed with a nurse bending over and smiling tenderly. I have never told anyone of this before this moment. I was afraid they would laugh at me.:

The experiences in the _Tibetan Book of the Dead_ are closely similar to Western near-death experiences and also to the shamanistic (American Indian) journeys and experimental psychotherapies. Such experiences await us only after death. Plato and William Blake told us: "We are, at this very moment, writing our own after-death drama", and that "We are, ourselves, the shapers of our souls' destiny" (or Karma). "It is our evolution as a soul, and some will have attained very little and must repeat this life."

In dying, the Tibetans say, "The soul passes into different realms, passing through tunnels of light, being filled with immense joy and profound love, meeting beings in subtle light bodies, who are familiar to the soul, and experiencing realms of intense color, sound...." Those who have had near-death experiences report all these happenings. Buddha asked, "Where does the fire go when all the fuel is used up?"

The experience will be different for all of us. Christians will have a Christian experience, a Hindu will have a Hindu experience, and an atheist will probably be terribly confused, for he believes only in himself.

A most outstanding case of life after death was F.W.F. Meyers in 1901. He gave pieces of a message to several mediums before he died to be fitted together into a message. The messages were extremely complex, involving many classical illusions in several languages. All received bits of the puzzle from a "communicator" who claimed to be Meyers. Few skeptics have ever had the patience to study them but the mediums involved. Put together, they became a message from Meyers.

Ealin Wilson makes reference to many men who felt alienated from every day life because they had experienced brief flashes of some wider and deeper kind of awareness. They felt they were trapped into Heidegger's "triviality of everydayness", which led to suicide or to the contraction of various diseases.

Wilson also speaks of our ability to conjure up the reality of some other time and place. (Bridie Murphy, in the 1950s, was an extreme example of this ability.)

Near-Death Experiences (NDE's)

In the mid-60s Raymond Moody began talking to patients who had apparently died and then returned to life. There was an amazing similarity to their experiences (as there is to today's near-death experiences)--the sensation of traveling down a tunnel and emerging into some warm, tremendous life force, which they relate as being "God".

For months and years afterward they experience a sense of marvelous insight into life and no longer fear death. They now have the "courage to live", and they radiate an inner awareness which is seen by many who come into contact with them. Wilson refers to this as "the eighth level of consciousness" and is a proof of "life after death". One man makes the lecture circuit telling others of his experiences

The belief that consciousness, or existence, survives after death is found in all the ancient and non-Western cultures, in their religions, philosophies, cosmologies, ritual practices and various elements of social organization. They are all united in the belief that death is merely a transition, or transfiguration, not our final end. We in the West believe consciousness is a functioning of the brain and that consciousness ends when the brain dies.

We feel others' beliefs are primitive fear, magical thinking, and superstition. We ignore The Tibetan Book of the Dead which is filled with stories of out-of-the-body experiences (OBEs). The work of Moody, Ring, Sabon, and Kubler-Ross verify these stories.

Kimberly Clark in Seattle became a believer when Maria, a patient, had a severe heart attack and two days later went into cardiac arrest. She was brought back quickly and days later talked to Clark, telling of finding herself outside, over the emergency room driveway, and later seeing a tennis shoe on a narrow ledge. Upon checking her story, Clark found the tennis shoe, and her story of the driveway was correct in every detail, though she arrived at the hospital unconscious and late at night. The only way she could have seen the shoe is if she were floating at very close range to it. It was enough evidence of an OBE for Clark.

The experience of the subtle light, (Christ to the Christians) is very pleasant, in fact blissful. At the next level, NDEs report they have never experienced anything as peaceful, as profound. In my own case, I had no fear of death because I knew I was not going to die. The dying experience and NDE are actually "Fun". (As reported, they fear death no more.) Once one gets over the terror of dying, the process is wondrous. When the descent begins (Bardo) or intermediate stages between two stages, one's karmic propensities, all of one's attachments, desires, fears, appear before one's eyes, just as in a dream, because the Bardo is a purely mental or subtle dimensional, dreamlike state, where everything one thinks appears as a reality.

This is never mentioned by those with NDEs for they are just tasting the early stages of the overall process. Most have never studied Tibetan Buddhism. In fact, they have never heard of it, but their experiences are essentially similar because it reflects the universal and cross-cultural reality of the "Great Chain of Being". It now appears there is simply no other way to read what has been accumulated in the NDE realm.

Buddha says, "We suffer in this life because we are not true to our essential nature which is goodness and whose evolution should be toward freeing that essential goodness.

"Every act which we perform for others is a step toward freeing this goodness. All our negative acts inhibit or obscure this trait." He also said, "If you want to know your past life, look into the state of your present life." This is the key to our future. The whole point is "not to be ashamed of oneself when you die."

When death is inevitable, as in incurable illnesses, great care must be taken to insure the dying person's peaceful frame of mind. It is most essential that they are not disturbed or distraught. A peaceful and loving atmosphere should be maintained, and an opportunity presented to make these last moments truly meaningful--a chance to ask forgiveness and to clear up unfinished business. (Kubler-Ross says unfinished business at dying is the hardest--the dying cannot let go.) The dying must abandon attachment which enables them to surrender at the moment of death.

"In an instant they are separated.

.In an instant, complete enlightenment"

Tibetan Book of the Dead

This reminds me about Earline's dog appearing to her in the horse barn. Before he appeared, the barn cat put her back and hair up and ran from the barn. She saw Earline's dog down by the stall of his favorite horse. The literature is replete with tales of where pets ran from rooms, have hidden under the sofa or tables, hackles up with the appearance of an apparition or ghost. It is impossible for one to entice them into a haunted room or part of a house where ghosts are seen. It would seem our pets have a greater avenue into the supernatural than we do.

CHAPTER VIII

GRIEF

He's dead! Oh! Lay him gently in the ground

And may his tomb by this verse renowned,

Here, Shock, the pride of all his kind is laid,

Who fawned like man, but ne'er like man betrayed.

John Gay--Elegy on Shock, A Lap Dog

Does Your Pet Have an Afterlife?

Cemeteries

Many animal shelters will handle disposal of pets, but they just take them to an incinerator which charges $5-$10 per animal. When animals are not claimed, the shelters "must foot" the disposal bill. Clinics are required by law to accept animals. In Farmington, Maine, in one year, six tons of animals were disposed of.

One hates to think their own pet could suffer such a fate. It's too heartbreaking to think about. Laws are becoming stricter, but I buried both Brandy and Kristen in the back yard where I could visit them every day and have grown flowers on their graves.

A pet is a member of the family, and you want the best for it when it passes away. To fulfill this need, pet cemeteries are springing up all over the U.S. One of the largest is in Biddeford, Maine, and over 6,000 pets have been interred since 1955. "It's a normal cemetery", says Florence Guidi, the owner, "except we don't embalm."

"Pets are buried by all kinds of people", said Mrs. Guidi. The farthest a pet traveled was from Caracas, Venezuela.

"We have taken to referring the more grief-stricken owners to a qualified therapist or grief counselor. No one, except those who have lost one of their own pets can understand this grief. It can be numbing and last for years."

Most animals buried are dogs and cats. There have been an increasing number of birds, parrots, rabbits, ferrets, and even raccoons and squirrels. Grief is not confined to humans: many dogs have been observed standing near their friends killed by cars.

Pine Ridge Cemetery

Poems and great tributes to pets have been written by Lord Byron, Elizabeth Barrett browning, and James Thurber among others. None has been any more heart-rending and filled with pain than those written in stone at the Pine Ridge Cemetery in Dedham, Massachusetts.

It is the oldest pet cemetery and rests on 27 rolling acres, carpeted and hushed by a deep layer of pine needles. The cemetery is run by a humane organization, and found here are touching tributes dating back to the turn of the century.

The beloved pets of Lizzie Borden, explorer Richard Byrd, and the conductor, Serge Koussevetzky are interred here. Every animal, from horses to hamsters, iguanas and ocelots, rests in these grounds and is memorialized, some by ornate tombstones.

There is "Heather, Queen of Scotties", and "Baby Buster Smith", "Crinkle Queensbury", and "Kettlewind Fritz", a dachshund of outstanding merit (1939-1952). The headstone of Dewey (1898-1910) is particularly poignant: "He was only a cat, but he was human enough to be a great comfort in hours of loneliness and pain". And there is "Trinket": "Blind, she saw with her heart".

Names like Rags and Checkers, Snuff, Bootie and Jiggs may have given way to Heidi, Ruby, Ginger, Kristen, Snowball and Bunny, but the feelings are the same. In the new part of the cemetery, Budweiser: "If my love could have save you, you would still be by my side. Now you are forever in my heart..." Also, there is a heart-shaped tombstone to His Majesty--Bear-Bear, whose inscription reads:

"January 6, 1956-January 12, 1971

A poodle was he

Although he never knew.

'Til we meet again

For Eternity

We love you"

What this cemetery tells us is that lavishing love on animals is nothing new and that ceremony and ritual can comfort us over the loss of a pet, as well as over that of a relative.

Jane Nathanson, a social worker and grief counselor, points out, "...the loss of a pet can cause pain more intense than losing a friend or relative. Our feelings are not conflicted toward our pets. We love them whole-heartedly and without reservation. No painful memories or frustrations cloud our feeling toward them. They are our true, understanding friends. Our love and our grief is pure."

Michael T. Thomas, who runs the cemetery, said about 300 animals are buried here every year. He says, "There's nothing you could do at a burial that I haven't seen. Clergymen have come and chamber music groups have played. The service can be a great comfort to the owners", he believes and said, "The pet-human bond is sometimes greater than the human-human bond." Even hardened criminals, condemned by society, such as Lizzie Borden, show a softer side. In a quiet corner lies Donald Stuart, Royal Nelson, and Laddie Miller, her dogs who outlived her. All are "Sleeping awhile".

There is a huge, iceberg-like stone devoted to Admiral Byrd's beloved Igloo. Igloo was a short-haired terrier who accompanied Byrd to Antarctica and back. "Igloo was more than a friend".

Even macho men feel pain at the loss of an animal. There is a large marker for police horse, Prescott: "Never in the history of the Boston Mounted Police has there been a nobler steed poised with such grace. Goodbye, old friend and comrade, until we meet again in the verdant pastures."

Place of Honor

Dale Dunning, a Pet Cemetery president, said, "My parrot, Yorkie and dachshund are in an urn in my china cabinet. They have a place of honor in my house. The cemetery has two crematoria. We put the ashes in an urn and the family can make its own arrangements. Some people keep the ashes in their urn for months before bringing them in to be buried. The grieving process is very slow. It takes time to say goodbye."

"The loss of a pet is very personal", said Debra Peterson, a grief counselor, "An animal cemetery is a wonderful way to memorialize your pet. It provides ritual and a way to celebrate your relationship. Grief is the hardest work I do, and the process has many stages", she said.

When Peterson's pet cat, Ray, died, she had a collage made of the six pets she has lost. At first she couldn't look at the pictures but, in time, "Your memory improves and you get through your grief. It's different for each person."

Paul Meyers, the custodian, says, "People only come by at intervals. They come often after a family tragedy. When something terrible happens, they remember their pets buried out here. Kids sixteen and eighteen will come out here to look up a pet, buried when they were three or four. Our biggest is Memorial Day just as it is at people cemeteries."

Many of the markers carry the inscriptions "Miss You", "Forever", "Till We Meet Again".

Colma

Colma, California is a gorgeous Bay Area Rapid Transit System stop recently connected to San Francisco. Most of its residents will not get a chance to use it--ever! Most of Colma's residents are dead.

In this 2.2 square mile necropolis, nicknamed the "City of Souls", is thought to be unique in all America. Colma is a whole town devoted to the departed, the dead outnumbering the living one thousand to one. Colma is the final resting place for more than a million souls.

Almost anyone who used to be anybody around here is buried here. Wyatt Earp, William Randolph Hearst, and a whole host of silent picture stars. Tina Turner's dog is buried here in the special Pet's Rest Cemetery. Her dog, Trixie, is reported to be buried in one of Tina's fur coats. There are over 100,000 pets buried here, many with elaborate monuments.

The town's founders, aware of the space problem in San Francisco, incorporated the cemetery in 1924. Many were executives in the cemetery industry, and they envisioned a great cemetery complex. Thousands of graves were opened in San Francisco and their residents reinterred in Colma. Seventy-five percent of Colma is graveyards, just like Forest Lawn in southern California

Oregon's Pet Cemetery

Fresh flowers mark Sheri Lyn's grave marker. The epitaph reads: "You are so beautiful". The Joe Cocker song always reminds Karen Ashbacker of Sheri Lyn. Bright flowers mark 24 more graves in the deep green grass. Nearby, soggy Christmas decorations wait to be picked up.

"She was just eight weeks old when we got her", Karen said. Now her dog, a Pomeranian/poodle mix, lies at the bottom of the hill in the Oregon Human Society Cemetery. "She was a member of our family", Karen says of Sheri Lyn who died two years ago. "The kids grew up with her."

"Yes, I believe in a hereafter", Karen Aschbacker says, "I know Sheri Lyn and I will see one another again. I have a very happy life, and I know we will be together again."

At the cemetery gate there is a monument to Bobbie of Silverton, the collie whose return trip from Indiana to Silverton, Oregon inspired the 1942 novel and film, Lassie Come Home.

Among its 3000 graves are three beige marble mausoleums built in the early 60s. There are two columbaria containing 896 crypts for ashes, about half of which are filled.

It's very difficult for one to express one's feelings for a pet. There is a bond that is forged over the years which is much greater than that we form with our fellow men. When Brandy died, some well-intentioned person said to me,

"She was just a dog; you can always get another one. The shelter has lots of dogs." I just looked at that person. There was no way I could make them understand what a loving, gentle, considerate friend my dog, Brandy, was. My love for her was so great that I still cry every time I think of what a remarkable being she was.

Welsh corgis have always been my first love. They have a strength of character not often seen in men and seem, like e.e. cummings, to intuitively grasp the meaning of giving. They, and other pets, are superior to man in coping with pain and love. No one has ever seen a dog feel sorry for himself, although he may show hurt feelings. (Cats often become miffed when left alone and urinate and defecate on the bed clothing, but they are merely angry.) Puppies, too, chew up things, even the furniture, when left alone. A friend said his dog chewed up the three cushions on his couch and scattered the feathers from one end of the house to the other. His wife promptly said, "Either the dog goes or I do". The dog went. (In later years after they divorced, he felt he should have kept the dog.) Pets take their pain stoically. Dogs who have lost a leg are soon seen getting along on three legs. In one case, an alpha female wolf reasserted her right as alpha, though she had lost a hind leg.

Few of us love one another as well as our pets love us, and they always forgive us, no matter what.

I'd rather have an inch of dog than miles of pedigree.

Josh Billings

CHAPTER IX

SAYING GOODBYE

My little old dog,

A heartbeat at my feet.

Edith Wharton

Waiting for the Inevitable Time

by Gay S. Gassair

I keep waiting for the first inevitable signs, the hesitant gait, the diminished hearing, the protrusion of a rib. She's eleven now, past the typical life span of her breed, and I expected we would come to these crossroads some time back. I had been through it twice before with my beloved and still-missed dogs. But this one, despite vets and AKC pronouncements, is defiantly youthful.

"She can still hear the crinkle of an M&M bag four rooms away. She can still snag a frisbee out of the air. She not only eats her own food but any extra that I can't eat. Carpet spills are quickly gobbled up, a late-stage bonus of a long life. She chases raccoons, snaps at hornets and inhales any microscopic kernel of affection I send her way.

"Her muzzle is laced with gray. Her résumé of ills include being hit by a car, meningitis, epilepsy, and murderous river rapids, but she remains improbably young. And so I wait. I plead with fate to let her die in her sleep as the two before her did. I so want to dodge that excruciating, unthinkable decision and that saddest, O my heart, of all goodbyes."

Putting Your Pet Down

I hate this phrase. It is commonly used. I like to think you're just saying "so long for a while".

One lady had a pet cat, Bailey. He was 13 years old and at the end of his days. She and Bailey shared a special relationship, and he had been "the favorite" of all the cats she had owned.

In the past she let her husband take the cats to the vet. This time she could not bear the thought of his going through this without her loving touch and her voice to soothe poor Bailey.

She told me, "Bailey's passing caused a grief I had never experienced before. But my knowing that there was no struggle, that he felt no pain, and to be able to remember how he purred to the very end, assures me I did the right thing by going with him.

"It was the kindest thing I could do for him. After the love and affection he gave to me, it was the very least I could do."

When a Pet Dies

Portland, Oregon: Mary Lewis writes: "In 1984 I rescued a dog from the shelter just before they were going to euthanize him. An hour more and it would have been too late. I wondered what I'd call this black and white dog happily bouncing on the passenger seat. Even thought I was only going to keep him a short while until I found a good home for him. I had to call him something-- Shep--that's a good name for a dog. I decided all good dogs are named Shep.

"Ten years later Shep was still with me, or rather with Madeline, my three and a half year old, who considers Shep hers.

"It was a hard winter for Shep this year. He had all the old dog symptoms: bad eyes, bad skin, bad hips, but he could always wag his tail for Maddy. One afternoon while Maddy napped, I took Shep for his last trip to the vets.

"When Maddy awakened, I made her a cup of chamomile tea and sat down to read her _A Funeral for Whiskers_, a book by child psychologist, Lawrence Balter.

"Together we read about Sandy and her cat, Whiskers, who gets very sick and her mother takes her to the vet. The vet calls them later to tell them Whiskers has died. I sat rocking Maddy as I told her Shep, like Whiskers, had

died. Balter had written the book as a framework for kids ages three to eight.
He says it comforts the child when you read to them.

"Our children have a hard time accepting the death of a pet (and adults do,
too). It is often the child's first experience with mortality, and they quickly
understand the same thing will happen to their parents. In Balter's book, Sandy
asks her mother, 'Is daddy going to die?' Her mother's comforting but honest,
'Daddy is too young and healthy, Sandy. He will be with us for a long, long
time. But all living things die some day.'"

Don't make up stories about their pet "disappearing", or "he went to sleep"
or "bought the farm". Tell your child the truth in a straightforward manner and
then discuss what dying means. Your child may be angry at his pet for leaving
him. Responses are varied. Deal with each. Acknowledge it, don't trivialize
it. Parents can lead their children through the whole experience by talking about
their own feelings and memories of the pet.

Lou Ann Pickering often comforts grieving children. "The talking has to
happen. The tears have to happen", she says, "then the grief can be healed.
Commemorate the animal. Look at pictures of them, recall the good, funny
times. Her father and I did this with Maddy and when she went to sleep that
night, she said. 'He was a good dog, wasn't he, Mommy?'"

Ranger, the Legendary Dog of Oregon

Portland, Oregon, November 27, 1994: Rites were held for seven-year-old
Ranger last week. A legendary Newfoundland, Ranger traveled all over the
world. He rescued people, found lost animals, located babies. He ran through
earthquake ruins in the Philippines and in California. He followed scents across
Mt.'s Hood, Baker and Shasta, and he paddled across raging rivers.

In fact, little existed that could keep the newfie mix from finding his quarry.
Until last week.

Something was wrong when Ranger awoke on Thanksgiving morning. His
hip was stiff, and he had trouble walking. The next day he was dragging his hip
behind him. He could barely walk. "He was in obvious pain. He was
uncomfortable and there was nothing we could do", said Harry Oates, Ranger's

owner and trainer. Ranger had been diagnosed with hip dysplasia, a painful, degenerative condition which strikes quickly.

So Friday afternoon Oates gave Ranger a steak, played his favorite game and took him on his last ride to the vet. "At 3:30 he gave me one of his sloppy kisses and then he died in my arms", Oates said, tears running down his face.

So ended the long sage of Ranger, the legendary search and sniffer, locater of babies and pets and missing people for the last seven years.

In addition, Ranger had shown his talents at over 1000 school assemblies. Now that Ranger has crossed the Rainbow Bridge in the sky, his friends, both human and canine, came to a memorial service in his honor.

The service was held at Portland's Parkrose Community Church on 106th Avenue, and law officers and search officers attended in their dress uniforms. One of their own had died. The 45-minute service was followed by a viewing of Ranger's many medals and awards and ranger's cremated remains.

Oates invited everyone to the service, saying, "Ranger was really the public's dog. One rescue I'll never forget: a man called down from the second floor of a burning building. Ranger jumped out of the car and ran into the billowing smoke-filled entrance. Five minutes later, he emerged with the man's arms around his neck and his body dragging behind. He was some piece of work, that dog."

The Surviving Pet

Lancaster, PA: I read the other day of the dog who never forgot his brother's death and has often laid by his grave. When he dies, his owner will bury him next to his brother.

A lady wrote, "My dog, Pepper, and my cat, Nuthin, have been raised together. When Pepper died eight years ago, Nuthin refused to come into the living room. She spent all her time on the pillow she had shared with Pepper.

"I had Pepper cremated. The ashes were delivered in a small box which I put on the bottom of the shelf of my bookcase. That night Nuthin came into the living room and sniffed around until she spotted the box. She then sat on top of it, purring. Later, Nuthin curled up at my feet in the bedroom for the first time since Pepper died. She seemed to know Pepper was home again.

"When Nuthin died last May, I had her cremated and the ashes put in the same blue urn with Pepper's. Today it sits on the bookcase, and no one knows what's inside. But I know they will always be together, and this fills my heart with happiness."

Kappy

Everyone who loses a pet faces a long period of grief. Here is the way one lady coped with the loss of her husband.

Shortly after her husband of 26 years passed away, his secretary sent her his last dictation.

"I curled up on the sofa and turned on my portable tape player to listen to his voice. No sooner had I turned on the tape when Kappy, our little dog, immediately came dashing down the stairs looking for her 'daddy' (they had been inseparable). She pawed at the tape recorder and cocked her head quizzically. Then she jumped beside me and covered my face with kisses, then rested her head on my chest. It was very emotionally comforting to us both.

"I played the tape often during the first weeks after he died, and Kappy's reaction was always the same. God Bless his thoughtful secretary."

Farewell to Scout

Hollowell, Maine: Phyllis Austin, the Senior Writer for the Maine Times, wrote: "Scout's life was a full cup." Scout, her pet of 15 years, who considered himself indispensable to the world, died of thyroid cancer at the end of March.

She recalls Rachel Carson writing about the death of her cat, Jettie. "I can hardly think of doing without him. His life was so intertwined with mine."

"Death always marks a passage, and Scout 'transcended his pain, falling softly out of his aged body and into the arms of heavenly grace'. He left with the assistance of Dr. Sue Chandinia, who had cared for him since birth.

"When a member of my family died recently, relatives gathered around the kitchen table to remember his life, to cry and to laugh. Scout's death was announced by NYNEX, given the geographical dispersal of his many friends. Scout's ears would flap happily if he could hear the words said about him.

"Scout had his idiosyncrasies. He nipped at people's feet, tried to gobble up children. He was so endearing people forgave his bad habits. Scout had an unusual attitude and bearing for his miniature size. He seemed to know from birth he had entered a marvelous place, and just being himself was all he had to do to have a splendid time. 'If you can't care for an old dog you can't care for an old person', someone said. When Scout began to fail I called upon that adage. I carried him up and down the stairs and attended to his increasing needs. One of his last signs was sleep so deep he seemed caught up in another dimension."

Flush, Elizabeth Barrett Browning's cocker spaniel, was said by Virginia Woolf to be in a similar mind: "the deep and dreamless sleep of old age".

"Scout's pain was too great for him to sleep that last day. The only time he stopped crying was when I held him in my arms. I bundled him in a blanket and took him for a 'walk' in the woods and down by the bay.

"In the days after his death, I have heard him bark and 'seen' him amble about the yard. I fight the urge to leave leftovers for him. The silence replacing the space occupied by Scout is enormous--a silence shared by everyone who has lost a beloved companion."

Scout was buried in a pine grove near four fox kits killed on the road. Phyllis lay him on a bed of pine needles and wrapped in a prayer cloth. This grave is near several animal paths so he is visited daily by foxes, deer, raccoons, crows, and cardinals.

"We are wedded now, not by union but by separation, just as Anne Rutledge and Abraham Lincoln were."

And now he's dead and there are

Nights when I think I feel him climb upon our bed

And lay between us and I'd pet his head,

And there are nights when I

Think I feel that stare and

I reach out my hand to stroke

His hair,

And he's not there.

Oh, how I wish it wasn't true.

Jimmy Stewart, Actor--Poem to Beau

Death Notices

Another lady who thinks as Phyllis Austin did wrote to a columnist.

"I received this in the mail a few days ago. It was a first for me. Here it is. Mrs. ----, is announcing the death of her dear Amanda, who had to be put to sleep at 3:30 p.m. on Monday, May 15, 1994, after giving her mistress sixteen years of pleasure. What do you think? The reaction in Fresno is varied."

"Dear Fresno,

"I think Amanda must have been a dearly loved pet, and her demise was the same as losing a member of the family. If the announcement served as closure for her, I see nothing at all to criticize."

Euthanasia

A Veterinarian's Point of View

"When I realize an animal is suffering in pain, I have to realize I'm facing a terminal situation. I have to do it, but I still get a cold feeling in the pit of my stomach when I push the plunger on the syringe. I try to have the owner or a technician with me at that moment. I feel as if I'm going down an elevator shaft inside. It's an odd and terrible feeling to look a creature in the eyes and it's alive. And as you are watching it, in an instant it dies. It's like blowing out a candle. I am not a hired killer. If someone is moving out of town and they decide, 'Hell, let's kill the dog', I will refuse to do it.."

There is a heated discussion about putting pets and humans to sleep when the end is near. Dr. Kervorkian figured in the arguments. One lady was very indignant, and said: How can you compare putting suffering animals out of their misery with human? Animals have no souls and for them death is final. Humans have souls, and the way we handle life's challenges-especially incurable illnesses--will decide our fate in the hereafter."

I answered her in Dear Abby's words: "Come Judgment Day, I believe we will be judged not on how we suffered and died but on how we have treated our fellow men and the lives we have lived."

(A thought: When you make out your will, add a provision to cover your pets. Often pets are shunted from one family to another and never have a chance to recover from their grief. Will them to someone who cares for them almost as much as you do. If I predecease Ruby, she will go to my friend, Richard Geil, who loves her almost as much as I do.)

A Caring Letter from a Vet (12/26/91)

Dear Susan:

I know how hard it was to let Abby go. She was a friend for such a long time. Her kidneys refused to detoxify and, when they stop, it is most difficult to get them started. It was hard but it was best for her.

I'm sure you will think of Abby often, that's as it should be. She was your very special friend. Take care,

> Robert Telluill
> Brewer, Main, Veterinary Clinic

He's dead! Oh! Lay him gently in the ground

And may his tomb by this verse renowned,

Here Shock, the pride of all his kind is laid,

Who fawned like man, but ne'er like man betrayed

John Gay--Elegy on Shock, A Lap Dog

CHAPTER X

LASTING MEMORIES

Pet Abuse

My Dear Lad

For a great true heart dwell

Within those years,

Tender, patient and brave,

And very wise,

And knows when I'm sick or sad,

And knowing, loved me all the more,

The dear lad.

His love is unquestioning,

High and very fine,

For this little dog of mine

I thank Thee.

Unknown

Brandy

My favorite place in Freeport, Maine in the 80's was changed in the early 90's when the owners sold their Bed and Breakfast and moved to New Mexico.

In their fifties, they were an unlikely romantic duo. They had been married for just two years. Bob is a handsome devil, and he left a trail of broken hearts as he moved across the country, never able to set down roots, that is, until he met Laura and quickly realized what had been missing in his life. They pooled their resources, moved to Maine and purchased the Captain Elliot B&B and quickly made a success of the enterprise. The were most charming to their guests, and they had an incredible return rate, something over 90%.

When I came along selling dried flower wreaths, Laura quickly took a shine to my Welsh corgi, Brandy, and Brandy to her. They simply adored one another, and we all enjoyed watching them. It was hard to tear Brandy away when it was time to go, so I stopped by often.

In July of 1987, Brandy was stricken with a deadly lymphatic cancer which quickly wasted away her once-healthy body. In the middle of August, my friend and landlady, Linden, took her to the vets to be euthanized, as I could not bear the pain. Linden's boyfriend, Tom, had been a grave digger in his college days, dug her grave, and no dog was ever placed in a nicer grave.

I don't know what I would have done at the vets, for as I wrapped Brandy in her blankets, I broke into uncontrollable sobs. I could not stop crying, and tears are running down my face as I write this. It has been ten years now, and I still miss Brandy very much and always will. She brought a dimension to my life which was heretofore lacking.

Months later I stopped by the Captain Elliott and burst into tears, telling Laura about Brandy. I apologized and she said, "What kind of man would you be if you didn't cry?"

I have never forgotten her kind words with which she followed: "You were very blessed to have had Brandy. Someday, you know, if we lead exemplary lives and are good persons perhaps God will let us come back as a dog."

Whenever I recall Brandy, I am reminded of James Langston Hughes' Eulogy. Hughes became famous when he left poems with the American poet, Vachel Lindsay, who was staying at a hotel where Hughes worked as a busboy. Lindsay read his poems at a reading that night, and overnight Hughes became the first famous black poet in the South.

Here is a paraphrase of his Eulogy:

Tell all Brandy's mourners

To dress in red--

'Cause there ain't no sense

In Brandy being dead

Farley

Followers of "For Better or Worse", the comic strip, were dismayed to see the family dog, Farley, die rescuing one of the children. "I can pinpoint the exact moment Farley died", said Susan Stanley, a reporter for the Portland Oregonian.

Ever since cartoonist-writer Lynn Johnston's fictional family joined the Oregonian pages, Susan had followed the strip, syndicated in 1800 newspapers. The father, John, is a dentist; the mother, Elly, an aspiring writer; Michael is off to the university; enduringly shy Elizabeth with her high-school crushes; and April, whose unplanned arrival caused much consternation. And Farley.

It's a family to love. The drama is usually low key, touching and amusing. One friend's son turns out to be gay, John gets grouchy at his office and sometimes is not too thoughtful. Elly is laid off at the library but lucks into a bookstore job. Not exactly high drama, but very dear to follow every day.

And Farley. He has aged. He's too old to sire any more puppies. (He's a big English sheepdog.) Then little April falls into a rain-swollen river and Farley goes in after her. (Susan broke into tears at this episode.) "What's the matter?", her husband asked.

"Farley's going to die."

"Farley. Who is Farley?" he asked.

"Well", and Susan explains the story line to him. "You know he's going to save her, but he's going to die", Susan sobbed.

"Maybe not, honey", her husband said. With heavy heart and lumped throat, Susan followed the unfolding adventure.

Young Edgar, Farley's son, alerts the family, and April and the dog are snatched from the jaws of death. Sort of. "Good boy, Farley, you're a hero", says the comic-strip father. Then Farley dies and is buried in a ravine. A few words are said about Farley being an old dog, and no one lives forever, and let's appreciate the ones we have, and the family moves on. They still have Farley in a way, in his son, Edgar.

Years ago a book editor told Susan, "Never kill a dog. Kill the grandmother, kill one of the kids, but never kill the dog. Readers will never forgive you."

Her words were prophetic. Lynn Johnston was deluged by letters from irate readers. She was forced to give a lengthy explanation about Farley's death. She said children have to come to terms with death. Nothing is permanent, especially with animals who have such short lives. Several letters warned her to keep her hands off Edgar.

A follow-up piece in the Houston Chronicle said: "The funnies are getting serious. In 'Luann', a teenage main character was seriously injured in a car wreck. The driver, her cousin, was drunk. The mother in 'Curtis' was assaulted near an ATM machine.

"In 'For Better or Worse', the beloved family pet, Farley, died after saving young April from the icy clutches of a raging river.

"Historically, strips have always been a mix of humor with a dash of realism. Farley's passing was a classic example of that.

"Reaction to Farley's death was extremely negative, and many readers sent complaining letters. Cartoonist Lynn Johnston said a desire for authenticity in part led to her reluctant decision to kill off Farley. 'The characters are all growing and developing in real time and have been for years', she said. 'If I'm going to be true to the strip, then Farley had to go. After all, Farley had aged considerably within the strip, and death was the next natural step', Johnston concluded."

Moles

We don't know much about moles. They spend their lives underground, aerating and tilling the soil and one seldom has had the joy to see one. Many people consider them a nuisance as they disrupt their manicured lawns. To them I say, "Get a life!" People who want manicured, flawless lawns should put in astroturf or hire Martha Stewart!

I will always remember a nature experience written by Louise Metcalf.

"Several years ago I opened our garage door and in scurried a small, very dark furry creature that immediately disappeared amongst our stored belongings.

About a week later I was again the garage basement area, when out walked the mole, seemingly slow and confused and, I was sure, hungry. I scooped him up with a box and covered it with a screen and put in some food and water, intending to return him to the woods later in the day.

I soon heard a strange, canary-like, high trilling. There was my mole, head lifted high, throat vibrating, a most beautiful sound coming forth. This went on for fifteen or twenty minutes without pause, while I stood there hearing but unbelieving. Then silence. I looked in and my little musical friend was lying dead."

Together in Life and Death

When Barnee Coffee died a few months ago, he was buried next to Minnie, the pet elephant he tended for 31 years until she died with cancer in 1992. Barnee told friends, "Some people will think I'm crazy, but Minnie and me were so close for so long. I cleaned her and nursed her like a baby when she was sick. She wouldn't eat or leave her stall unless I was there with her. This sweet, gentle lady was all I ever had in this world. I wanted to be with her on the other side" (of the Rainbow Bridge).

His friends took Barnee to the cemetery and buried him beside Minnie.

ABUSES

Dog Killers

Lynwood, WA, July 1994:   A Mt. Vernon, Washington man has collected $8,000 for the loss of a dog that was deceptively obtained and then sold and later killed for research at the University of Washington.

"To our knowledge, this is the first time a laboratory animal deal has been subjected to civil prosecution and civil damages", said Michael Fox of the Animal Welfare Society.

Don Johnson ran an ad in 1989 seeking a good home for his dog, Sasha. He selected Don and Judee Peters of Monroe, who promised him Sasha would have the run of their farm for as long as he lived.   Later, Johnson found out in a PAWS newsletter the Peters were licensed by the U. S. Agriculture Department as Class B research animal dealers. Johnson was very upset, as he originally had rescued Sasha from an abusive home.

Documents obtained by PAWS showed Sasha had been sold by the couple to the University about a week after they took the dog from Johnson. The animal was killed in a lung injury experiment two weeks after he arrived at the school.

PAWS' attorney, John Casto, filed suit against the Peters soon afterwards alleging fraud and breach of contract. When the Peters failed to dispute the allegations, a court commissioner awarded Johnson $10,000 in damages, and a judgment was automatically placed against the couple's property.

The damages went uncollected until early July 1994 when Johnson agreed to an $8,000 settlement. PAWS and Johnson had gone to the legislature in 1989 who, in turn, made it a class C felony to obtain a dog or cat for research by theft or deception. Johnson also blames the University of Washington for using pets in biomedical research. The University researcher, Dr. Gerald Van Hoosier, agreed. "Even if one pet is used for research, that is one too many", Van Hoosier pointed out "The University had worked with PAWS in 1989 on the Pet Protection Act. Our school deals only with established dealers", Van Hoosier said, and reports any questions about an animal's origin to the USDA immediately and keeps a detailed file along with photographs of all research animals.

Any animal determined to be a pet is immediately returned to his owner unless the owner gives it to the Medical School", Dr. Van Hoosier concluded.

Artist Faces Jail for ShootingDogs

Raton, New Mexico, January 5, 1996: An Eagle Nest man faces jail time for shooting two dogs whom he said were disturbing his sleep. Timothy Grieb, an artist who sometimes works at the Angel Fire ski area, woke up one night last June to his neighbor's barking dogs, grabbed his rifle and repeatedly shot the dogs in the head. "It was pretty gruesome", said Assistant DA, Leslie Fernandez. Grieb must choose next month whether to serve six consecutive months in the Colfax County jail or spend every weekend of the next year in the jail. He also must pay either $2,500 in fines or donate $1,000 to the Raton Humane Society.

Fernandez said Grieb must also pay $500 in restitution to his neighbor, Katie Davis. "Grieb pleaded guilty in November to a misdemeanor charge of malicious slaughter of domestic animals and to a petty misdemeanor charge of negligent use of a deadly weapon", said Casey Irwin of Raton, Grieb's attorney.

Orangeburg, SC: A man who shot and killed a champion hunting dog, Ranger, while it was treeing a raccoon, must pay the owner $10,000 and serve five years' probation.

Samuel Claymoor said he shot Ranger in January because he thought Ranger was going after his hogs. He pleaded guilty last week to a dog-killing charge and apologized to Ranger's owner.

Clyde McGinnis said he was training his six-year-old treeing Walker hound in January for the Great American Coon Hunt. "He was a dog of a lifetime. He had a bark you could hear long after the dogs got so deep in the woods you couldn't hear the average dog", McGinnis said. "I'm going to miss Ranger and doubt if I'll ever find another one like him."

CHAPTER XI

HEROES

Nay, brother of the sod

What part hast thou in God?

What spirit art thou of?

It answers, "love".

Katherine Lee Bates

War Dogs

Washington, D.C.: A lifesized, black and gold sculpture of a Doberman was unveiled in Washington recently. The sculpture honors the hundreds of dogs who gave their lives to save U.S. troops during WWII.

"The monument, the first to honor the heroic canines, will be transported to the pacific island of Guam where it will stand guard over the official dog cemetery at the U.S. Naval Base at Orote Point", officials said.

It is a part of the commemoration of the 50th anniversary of the liberation of Guam. The battle lasted from July 21 to August 10, 1944, and claimed the lives of 6,900 marines and army soldiers, and an estimated 18,500 Japanese.

The dogs, whose duties included leading landing parties and exploring caves to ferret out the hidden Japanese also served as sentries. "They saved hundreds of lives on Guam alone and many more hundreds on other captured islands", said Lt. General Claude M. Kicklighter. Ninety percent of the dogs used in the Pacific Island campaigns were Dobermans.

islands", said Lt. General Claude M. Kicklighter. Ninety percent of the dogs used in the Pacific Island campaigns were Dobermans.

Love and Loyalty

Fargo, ND: A three-year-old collie named Papillion saved a little baby's life. The baby had vomited up her milk and was choking to death. Papillion ran to the bathroom where the mother was taking a shower, pulled back the shower curtain, jumped up on the side of the tub and barked furiously. The mother ran to the baby's crib. The baby's lips were turning blue. She called 9ll. The rescue squad responded in less than two minutes and cleared the baby's throat so that it could breathe.

"She saved my baby's life", the grateful mother repeated over and over.

Cutler, Montana: Out checking his cattle ranch, Jim Bartelson was thrown from his horse, and his leg was broken in four places. Hustler, his big Shepherd mix, stayed by his side the whole night and drove off three coyotes who tried to attack the helpless Bartelson. Hustler chased them away time and time again. The next morning his wife called the sheriff's office and a search party was organized. They found him nine hours later, faithful Hustler by his side.

Springfield, MO: The night Michelle Austin crawled into bed, she never realized she was soon to face death. At three the next morning, she was awakened by the frantic barking and pawing of her dogs, Lady and Popeye. She awoke to a smoke-filled room and could see crackling flames in her hallway. She grabbed Popeye in her arms but couldn't find Lady, who had been overcome by the smoke. She went out the side window just as the rear end of the house burst into flames. The firemen found little Lady's body under Michelle's bed the next afternoon.

Ft. Lauderdale, FL: The owner of a dog in Ft. Lauderdale, Florida buried her nine puppies in the back yard. A macho man, he had often preached, "I don't believe in having my dog spayed". Sheba, the mother, found the spot and unearthed the puppies, three of whom were already dead. The other six survived and were taken to an animal shelter. Her owner has been charged with three counts of animal abuse under the Ft. Lauderdale Animal Abuse Act. He could be sentenced to fifteen years in jail under the terms of the 1989 Act.

Oklahoma Bombing

Harry Oakes's dogs are trained to yelp when they find bodies after a disaster. Four days after the Oklahoma City bombing, they howled the gruesome news of the young, innocent victims.

Oakes was called in by Federal disaster authorities. "Around the nursery area of the building, the dogs gave nothing but death alerts", Oakes said. In an early morning sweep, Valerie, a border collie, and Quigley, a mixed breed, found the remains of four children trapped in the second-floor day-care center.

"The dogs worked in two-hour shifts", said Oakes, who has trained search dogs for 23 years. Valerie and Quigley are the two best he has ever had. "The dogs have to take breaks because their work depresses them. Their tails go way between their legs when it's time for a break", he said.

Oakes flew into Oklahoma City from Portland, OR, with his partner, Becky Nimomo, to relieve other dogs and trainers.

Before the building was blown up and destroyed, the dogs found 165 out of the 168 victims. The remaining three were unearthed by bulldozers.

Cookie

Peoria, IL: During a slow period, Pete Johnson had been laid off by Caterpillar, the tractor company, during the slow period. Running out of money, Peter took a room at an old, shabby, run-down hotel for $8 a week. No pets were allowed but he sneaked Cookie, his cocker mix, into his room. Cookie was the only reminder of his beloved wife who had died some three years earlier.

One December morning at 4:30, Peter awoke to find Cookie sitting on his chest pawing his face and barking loudly. He smelled smoke and jumped out of bed. He opened his door to find the corridor slowly filling with the gray-white death.

Peter grabbed Cookie in his arms and ran down the hall pounding on doors, alerting the sleeping tenants. He handed Cookie to someone outside the hotel and ran back in to alert the second- and third-floor residents. Everyone got out safely, but Peter and four others suffered smoke inhalation.

The mayor of Peoria and the fire chief presented Pete with the year's award for bravery and, asked to give a speech, Peter reached down and took Cookie into his arms, saying, "This is your real hero, not me".

Cool Head Under Fire

<u>Denver, Colorado, July 6, 1996</u>: Almost any dog will wake you if there's a fire. But how many will open a door, jump a fence and squeeze through a doggy door made for a dog five times smaller? At least one.

Cody, a 55 pound wild herding dog, did just that when he spotted a garbage bin burning behind the home of his lady love, Stempy.

"It's just like Rin-Tin-Tin or Lassie or something", said Stempy's owner, Linda Van Auker. Van Auker said a noise awakened her in her southwest Denver home at 1:30 a.m.

"I thought someone was in my home", she said. "I got up and looked, and there was Cody."

Cody, who lives across the street, is a frequent visitor to her home. Stempy, a ten-pound miniature dachshund, is the chief reason he drops, by Van Auker said. But Van Auker thought the hour was a bit too late, definitely past Stempy's curfew. So she ordered Cody back home.

As he departed through the tiny doggy door, she heard someone banging on the front door. A neighbor shouted there was a fire in the back yard.

Van Auker called 911. Then she looked out the back door and saw four-foot flames dancing above a trash bin in the alley behind her house. "That's when I realized what Cody was doing.", she said.

Cody's owner, Gordon Gideons, slept through the drama. When he awakened the next morning, Cody was asleep on the floor in his usual place, the door firmly closed.

Stray Dogs Save Boy's Life

<u>Springfield, MO, March 3</u>: They led a boy to the brink of death and then saved his life. Now the dogs have been rewarded with a new home.

Josh Carlisle, a ten-year-old with Down's syndrome, was playing in his yard when a pair of wandering dogs caught his eye, and he followed them into the rugged, wooded Ozarks near his home.

For three days as temperature hovered in the single digits, up to 350 volunteers searched for the boy. On Saturday, a man on horseback heard dogs barking and found Josh in the company of two protective dogs.

"The dogs took care of him as if they were his mothers", Sheriff Ralph Hendrix said Monday. "They probably curled up to him all night long to keep him warm--warm enough to stay alive for us to find him."

The dogs are "God's angels", said Josh's stepfather, Lynn Coffey. He and Josh's mother, Johnny Coffey, planned to give the strays a new home as their reward.

Fang

In Sarasota, Florida, a four-foot-long, black poisonous water moccasin slithered into the back yard of a home where a two-year-old child was playing. The snake struck the toddler's pants, but its fangs could not penetrate the denim of his coveralls.

At that moment, the family dog, a small Chihuahua, a three-pound acquisition from the local animal shelter, grabbed the snake in its jaws and yanked and yanked on the snake's head and pulled the snake away from the baby's coveralls. The mother, alerted by the dog's barking, came running and clubbed the water moccasin to death.

"Fang" (as they renamed him) was lauded as the family hero and became the pride of the neighborhood, and adoptions at the shelter skyrocketed.

Tiree and Tara

Innisfel, Ontario: It was well below zero when dog trainer, Jim Gilchrist, took his pets--Tiree, a golden retriever, and Tara, a rottweiler--out for their afternoon walk in February 1995. As they crossed frozen Lake Simcoe, Gichrist felt the ice give way. The dogs had bounded ahead. When they looked back, Gilchrist was floundering in the water. Tara rushed over and, when the ice gave way under her, joined Gilchrist in the ice-filled water.

Wise Tiree crouched on her belly and crawled to the hole where Gilchrist grabbed on to her collar. Tara climbed up on Gilchrist's back and made it to the firm ice. She then laid on her belly alongside Tiree so Gichrist could grab her collar with his other, free hand. The dogs crawled forward dragging him free from what could have been his icy grave.

When they got home, all three took a hot bath. "They deserved it", said a grateful Gilchrist. Since the incident he has grown even closer to his dogs. "You can converse with Tara like a human being", he said, "and if you tickle Tiree under the chin, she'll follow you anywhere."

Norman

In Seaside, Oregon, Annette McDowell's favorite pastime is strolling along the nearby Necanicum River with husband, Larry; son Larry, Jr., two and one-half; and their four-year-old yellow lab, Norman. Norman is blind from a retinal infection but still enjoys being in the water. In fact, he lives for the family's trips to the beach.

During a walk last July 15, Norman ran off and refused to come when Annette called him. "He looked like he was on a mission", she said. That proved to be true.

Minutes earlier, Lisa Nebley and her younger brother, Joey, 12, tourists from Washington state, found themselves caught in one of Oregon's infamous rip tides. Joey managed to swim broadside to the current and reach the shore. Lisa's screams had alerted Norman, and he was off to the rescue.

Norman finally reached Lisa who grabbed onto his tail, and the two headed back to the shore. "I don't know how much longer I could have lasted", Lisa said, hugging Norman.

When Lisa's mother, Elaine, heard of the rescue, she "started shaking and crying", being consoled by Lisa's father, Jeff. Today, an enlarged photo of Norman graces the wall of Lisa's bedroom alongside all those of her friends. "He's my guardian angel", Lisa said, smiling.

Corgis

There is a tale which is repeated often in the Queen of England's circle. As we all know, the Queen is devoted to her Pembroke Welsh corgis. Some years back during one of England's fierce February storms, the creek near Welsh corgi "Ellie's" home became a raging flood. Ellie's son, R. C. , dashed happily into what he had kown as a shallow creek.

He panicked and started swimming rapidly downstream, away from shore. Bobby Morris, the dog's owner, panicked also and jumped into the raging creek. She was dressed in heavy clothing which soon became waterlogged in the chest-high water.

Bobby began to scream hysterically. "I thought I was watching my puppy drown, and then I was drowning." Ellie, who has a cat-like dread of water, jumped in to save her master and her son. She swam right to Morris.

With Ellie in her arms, Morris was once again able to think rationally. When she began to think clearly, R.C. began to think clearly as well, and swam right to his mother, and all three made it safely to shore.

Ellie is often used in therapy treatment with withdrawn patients. The people who know Ellie tell many different tales about her now-legendary qualities. One of the funniest concerns is her AKC registered name which is-- Lost Hills Ellie Oop.

Millie

Marge Dakin looked up from her desk at the animal shelter. Before her was a lady with a basket of six puppies and an anxious mother dog looking up at her. The dog's name was Millie, and her owner told Marge, "I just can't afford to keep her any longer." There were tears in her eyes.

Marge took Millie to her new home in the back kennel. Within days the shelter knew they had a remarkable resident. No one had ever seen a mother take better care of her puppies. As the last of them was adopted, eight more puppies arrived whose mother had been killed by a car. Millie immediately took them to her ample bosom and raised them as her own.

In the next two years, Millie raised two more orphaned litters, three baby raccoons, five fox kits, and a couple of baby squirrels. Tales of Millie's mothering spread far and wide in the shelter community.

One day a lady arrived at the shelter wanting to adopt Millie. She lived on a large 600-acre farm and had many, many animals. She needed someone like Millie to look after them. The shelter readily agreed.

The last we heard, Millie was busily caring for baby sheep, goats, chicks, and even a gaggle of geese. She is especially partial to baby lambs.

Edie

Mention pit bulls to people and their eyes glaze over and a look of fear becomes apparent. Pit bulls are not all bad, as the following tale illustrates:

When a pregnant border collie was brought to the animal shelter in Longview, Washington, volunteer coordinator, Karla Dudley, asked Melanie Mills to house her and care for the puppies. Last year Mills had taken in some of the rottweilers in the infamous Ingrid Pearson abuse case where 80 dogs were confiscated.

Although all the eight collie puppies survived, the mother died from an advanced case of liver cancer. Mills is the owner of Edie, a grand champion American pit bull terrier. Edie took the puppies to her bosom and carefully cared for them, keeping track of all eight when she returned from outside. She cleaned each of them every day. If one was being hand fed by Mills, Edie checked to see that the puppy was there. Though not lactating at that time, Edie soon began to produce milk to nourish the puppies.

Mills laughs as she watches Edie and says, "Edie is so gentle; she thinks they are award-winning pups. She is sure they are going to get the brindle stripes and be regular pit bulls any day now."

Quick to defend pit bulls, Mills says, "They have a bad reputation because they have irresponsible owners. These owners have dogs who end up at the humane shelter." Karla Dudley agrees.

"We're all working together on this one", Dudley says. "Unlike humans with their built-in prejudices, dogs just don't have any boundaries. When the puppies are grown, we'll find good homes for them.

Edie, whose champion name is Yankee Pride Cover Girl, will be sad when that day arrives. She is clearly enjoying her foster mother's role.

Karma

Gig Harbor, Washington, September 1997: Eddie Hilliard cashed in all his earned human karma last week. We was awakened last Saturday night to his dog Karma's barking. Almost overcome by smoke, he found the living room was ablaze.

"Had it not been for her, I wouldn't be here," said Hilliard, 49, hugging his golden retriever around the neck. "She knows she's a hero."

Hilliard is so grateful that in addition to rewarding Karma with steaks and doggie treats, he plans to nominate her for this year's "Dog Hero" award. He is also sending money to the Humane Society in her name.

"I told her she's going to be the hero of the year. She'll be right up there with Lassie and Rin-Tin-Tin", said the exuberant owner.

Rusty (and other blessed creatures)

Andrea Wall knew she had an exceptional dog when Rusty scooted across the floor on his belly and then laid, tummy up, before a little girl. Rusty had sensed the little girl's fear of dogs, and this was his way of telling her not to be afraid of him. Andrea is a 14-year volunteer with the Oregon Humane Society.

She had brought Rusty to the special Grotto meeting to bless the animals as an example of a social therapy dog. Rusty has had special training to assist Andrea in her work as an occupational therapist. She told the assembled animals lovers how Rusty, a mostly border collie, literally jumps through hoops the stroke victims hold up to strengthen their arm muscles.

Rusty earned the thanks of a family when he went to visit a comatose man in a nursing home. The family knew he was dying and hoped for one last talk with him. At first the man showed no sign of change. Then Rusty jumped into bed with the man and nuzzled his hand. The man began to pet Rusty as the family began to cry. The man then opened his eyes to see his family gathered around him.

"Seeking blessings is as important for animals as it is for people", Wall said. Her friend, Myrtle Wood, brought two long-haired cats in to this special service. Beethoven and Bomberina have helped many patients understand the benefits of spiritual maintenance for themselves and others.

Marie Gascon brought her greyhound, Blue, along with her great-granddaughter, Tamarra, whom Blue guards as if she were her puppy, a truly symbiotic relationship. Gascon held Sparky, a silky terrier, in her arms, another dog to be blessed this special day.

"I bring my pets every year to the Grotto to be blessed", she said, "I love them and want them to be safe."

Midnight

Bernita Rogers and her husband had seen their share of family tragedy. Three babies had died at childbirth, so when their fourth child, Stacey, was born healthy the couple were very happy. "Needless to say, she was pretty special to us", said Bernita.

When Stacey was five months old, she came down with a cold, and the doctor suggested a humidifier for her room. A week later, as Bernita tried to nap in the next room, the family cat, Midnight, wouldn't let her. She clawed at her leg, jumped on her lap, and acted very strangely. Then Bernita heard a moan from the nursery, and Midnight rushed in and jumped up on the dresser. The baby was blue and gasping for air. They rushed her to the hospital where she was resuscitated from respiratory failure and was diagnosed as having a viral infection. "If it weren't for Midnight, Stacey would have been a crib death."

Now ll, Stacey lives with her parents in Kansas City, where she is a healthy fifth grader. Midnight, now 13, still looks after her. "She mostly lies in the sun now", Bernita said, "I think she can do it all day long."

Angie

We've all read and heard of dogs barking and waking their owners when the house caught fire. Few can top the story of Sandy Shawn. She was roused from her sleep by her pet angelfish. She and her three daughters would probably have died in their house fire if Angie hadn't jumped out of her bedside tank and landed on Sandy's face. "I was instantly awake and found the bedroom filling with smoke and flames were licking at the foot of our bed. I'm just thankful she did, and I had the presence of mind to put her back in her tank."

Downy

Tanya Birch in Wisbech, England, considers Downy, her pet rabbit, to be a hero. Smoke and flames awoke the bunny rabbit, and Downy hopped into the room where Tanya was sleeping. "He began to scratch my bedside table, and the noise woke me", she said. "I saw the smoke and flames all around. I grabbed Downy and fled through my open window just before my bedroom exploded in flames. I was able to alert two other families who also owe their lives to my little hero."

Falco

It is said a writer can find a story no matter where he is. I recently completed my sixteenth and last, I hope, cross-country trip. I drove a 1985 Nissan Sentra which had given me trouble in the past. This time it decided to vapor-lock, a disease which causes the engine to seize up, you lose all your engine compression, and the car stops dead.

Leaving North Platte, Nebraska where I stopped for gas the engine vapor-locked crossing a bridge in the busiest section of North Platte. As I put up the hood, the universal distress signal, a new police Bronco pulled up in back of me.

The officer's name was Mark P. Stokey who told me they had the same trouble before their police vehicles had fuel injection. He told me he would stay there until I could get going. With all the traffic whizzing by, I really appreciated his kindness.

I soon noticed he had a police dog in back, and we got to talking about these amazing dogs. Falco was his dog. He'd had him since he started his police work, in 1989, and will care for him when he retires next year, as he has a bad hip.

Falco was weaned and trained in Europe and was purchased for $6500 when he was three. Prevailing thought at that time was dogs would not be effective at an earlier age. Today the Nebraska State Police use dogs as young as age one and find them to be equally capable of doing the job.

Falco is the most famous dog in all of Nebraska. During his career he has sniffed out two and a half to three million dollars worth of cocaine and marijuana. Among his startling finds were marijuana in a tool box, a kilo of cocaine found in a hidden compartment of a truck, and two and one-half pounds of marijuana found in a freezer. He has also apprehended a car thief by chasing him down and holding him at bay until Officer Stokey arrived.

Today with drugs arriving in the stomachs of people, sewn into exotic animals and hidden in false bottoms of poisonous reptile cages and boxes of spiders, the police drug squads in America are kept busy employing specially trained dogs like Falco.

When Officer Stokey isn't busy tracking down drug dealelrs, he employs Falco in another capacity--therapy--by entertaining senior citizens in rest homes. Everyone is happy when Falco arrives. All too often our senior citizens are neglected by their families and rarely have visitors. Falco has become a bright spot in their dark, lonely days.

Falco has his own baseball card. It's put out by the Association of Nebraska Law Enforcers. The card shows Falco lying down, his police badge proudly displayed on his collar. The card was sponsored by T. O. Hass Tire, the Goodyear tire distributor in North Platte.

CHAPTER XII

HUNTING--ITS ADVOCATES

A hunter is a man who will spend all day in a duck blind and then when he returns home, complain if dinner is late.

Anon

The Englishman trots as he fox hunts, over hedges, through ditches and over streams and rivers, through waiters, saxophones, to the victorious finish; and who goes home depends on how many can fit in the ambulance.

Edna St. Vincent Millay
Recalled on her death, 19 October 1950

Some violent spectacle is normal in most countries (bullfighting as compared to boxing in the U.S.) and fox hunting in England (and cock fighting in Mexico).

Luis Gonzalez Seara

Quarry mine, blessed am I
In the luck of the chase
Comes the deer to my singing
Navaho Prayer

Try the brook that none esteem;
Do not fish the famous stream.
Guiterman--A Poet's Proverbs

When a big game hunter disappears you can bet something he disagreed with--ate him.   *Anon*

Women never look so well as when one returns wet and dirty from a day of hunting.   *Anon*

I have known a fox who was absolutely, passionately devoted to hunting--
after we had hunted him many seasons, I regret to say, we killed him.

> *Col. Sir Lancelot Rolleson, D.S.O.*
> *Quoted by M. Bateman in the MAIL*

Without foxes, there would be no hunting. And I'm afraid many would not
be able to make it through an English winter.

> *Anon in Horse and Hounds*

It isn't mere convention. It's plain to see those who hunt are the right ones
and those who don't, the wrong ones.

> *George Bernard Shaw*
> *Heartbreak House--1920*

Spirits of well-shot woodcock, partridge, snipe
Flutter and bear him up the Norfolk Sky.
> *John Betjamin*
> *Death of King George V*

Proud Nimrod first the bloody chase began
A mighty hunter
and his prey was man.
> *A. Pope--Windsor Forest*

...Here he lies where he longed to be
Home is the sailor, home from the sea
And the hunter home from the hill.
> *R.. L.. Stevenson--Requiem*

Man is the hunter,
Woman is his game
> *A. L. Tennyson--The Princess*

Kathleen Mavourneen!
The horn of the hunter
Is heard on the hill
Oh! Hast thou forgotten this day
we must part?
It may be for years
It may be forever...

Julia Crawford
Kathleen Mavourneen--1835

The world is made up of two classes--the hunters and the hunted.

Richard Connell
The Most Dangerous Game--1924

The hare, the partridge and the fox must be preserved first--so that they may be killed later.

John Lubcock
Pleasures of Life--1887

The Prince is a mighty hunter. I wonder why Englishmen must always want to be killing something.

H. S. Merriman--The Sowers--1896

What shall we go out and kill today?--was the breakfast inquiry. The Englishman's idea of happiness is having something to kill and then to hunt it.

Vincent Lean--Collectanea--1902

The hunter follows that which
flees him; taken, he leaves them;
and ever seeks what is beyond
what he has found.

Ovid--Amores--13 B. C.

Hunting has as much pain as pleasure.

Thomas Fuller
Gnomologia--1732

There commeth greater pleasure in the hunting than in the eating.

John Lyly--Euphues--1580

Taking random shots at crows with clods and potsherds.

Persuis--Satires--58 A.D.

His anger led him on 1000 wild goose chases.

Beaumont and Fletcher
The Pilgrim--Act 3--1621

You can't teach old sports like him new tricks.

Brete Harte--Two Men of Sandy Bar
(Harte is referring to old pigeon-shooting sports.)

Don't think to hunt two hares with one dog.

Ben Franklin--Poor Richard

What he hit is history.
What he missed is mystery.

Thomas Hood
referring to a guest's hunting stories.

T'is folly to take unwilling dogs out to hunt.

Anon

Huntsmen rest! Thy chase is done.

Sir Walter Scott
Lady of the Lake

Back limped with slow and
crippled pace
The leaders of the chase.
Ibid

Oh, Sir Thomas Lucy
Your venison is juicy
Juicy is your venison
Hence I apply my benison.
Shakespeare applying a benediction upon Sir Thomas Lucy who once prosecuted and fined him for poaching his game.

The birds seem to think the muzzle of my gun is their safest position.
Sidney Smith--1832

There is a passion for hunting, something deeply implanted within the human breast
Charles Dickens--1840

Queen and huntress, chaste and fair
Now the sun is laid to sleep
Seated in thy silver chair,
State in wonted manner keep:
Hesperus entreats thy light
Goddess, exceedingly bright
Ben Johnson
Cynthia's Revels--1600

The dusky night rides down the sky,
And ushers in the morn
The hounds all join in glorious cry,
The Huntsman winds his horn
And a-hunting we will go.
Henry Fielding--1734

And a-hunting we will go.
                              Henry Fielding--1734

   We tended to imagine Canada as a kind of vast hunting preserve for the
United States.
                              Edmund Wilson--A Piece of My

Mind

                    Bye Bye baby bunting
                    Daddy's gone a-hunting
                    Gone to get a rabbit skin
                    To wrap the baby bunting in.
                              Anon
                              Bye Baby Bunting

                    There were three jolly huntsmen
                    As I heard them say
                    And they would go a-hunting
                    On St. David's Day.
                    All day they hunted
                    And nothing did they find
                    But a ship a-sailing
                    A-sailing in the wind.
                              Anon--Three Jolly Huntsmen

                    As flies to wanton boys, we are to the gods;
                    They kill us for their sport.
                              Shakespeare--King Lear

CHAPTER XIII

HUNTING--ITS ADVERSARIES

My book, *Riel and Tillie,* stated my views on hunting--it is obscene! Here are a few of the opinions which parallel mine:

Historically wild animals have never killed for sport. Man is the only animal to whom the torture and death of his fellow creatures is amusing in itself.
> *James Anthony Froude--Oceana*

It is very strange and very melancholy that the paucity of human pleasures should persuade us to call hunting one of them.
> *Samuel Johnson--Miscellanies--1760*

Hunting was the labour of the savages of North America, but the amusement of the gentlemen of England.
> *Ibid--Johnsoniana--1765*

I cannot comprehend when I see a noble deer how educated and refined people can take pleasure in chasing it to death.
> *Heinrick Heine--German Poet*

He did not know a keeper is only a poacher turned inside out, and a poacher a keeper turned outside in.
> *Charles Kingsley--The Water Babies*

> I was a stricken deer which left the herd
> Long since: with many an arrow deep infixed,
> My panting side was charg'd when I withdrew
> To seek a tranquil death
> In distant shades
> > *W. Cowper--The Task--1780*

A herd abandoned deer,
Struck by the hunter's dart.

Shelley--Adonais

When a man wants to murder a tiger he calls it sport. When the tiger wants to murder him, he calls it ferocity.

George Bernard Shaw
Maxims for Revolutionists

Walk softly March
Forebear the bitter blow
Her feet within a trap
Her blood upon the snow
The four little foxes
Saw their mother go--
Walk softly.

Lew Screed--1919

Hunting their sport, plundering game was their trade,
In arms they ploughed, to battle still prepared.
Their soil was barren, and their hearts were hard.

Vergil--31 B.C.--The Aeneid

Good and much company and a good dinner; most of the discourse was on hunting, a dialect of which I know little.

S. Pepys--Diary--22 Nov. 1663

He thought at heart like a courtly Chesterfield, who, after a long chase o'er hills, dales, bushes, and what not, though he rode beyond all price, ask'd next day if, "Men ever hunted twice?"

Byron--Don Juan--Canto XIV

Soe that courageous Hart doth fight with Fate and calleth up all his might and standeth stout, that he may fall Bravle, and be avenged of all nor like a craven yield his Breath Under the Jawes of Dogges and Death.

Thomas Hood--Fall of The Deer

Hunting now has the idea of quality about it and is become the most important business in the life of a gentleman. Anciently it was quite otherways. Mr. Fleury has severally remarked that this extravagant passion for hunting is a strong proof of our Gothic extraction and shows an affinity of humour with the savage Americans.

John Dryden
Preface To The Pastoral of Vergil--1673

There are no wild animals until man makes them so.
Mark Twain

O barbarous man! Your cruel breasts assuage,
Why vent ye on the generous steed your rage?
Does not his services earn your daily bread?
Your wives, children, by his labours fed.
John Gay--Trivia--Book III--1720

Detested sport!
That owes its pleasure, to another's pain!
S. Cowper--The Task

The urge to kill, like the urge to beget
Is blind and sinister. Its craving is set
Today on the flesh of the hare;
Tomorrow it can
Howl for the flesh of man!
A. Vorznesenski--Hunting a Hare

I cannot think this creature died
By storm, or fish, or sea-fowl harmed
walking the sea so heavily armed.
(Or does it make for death to be
oneself a living armory?)
Andrew Young--1968--The Dead Crab

God made all the creatures and gave them
Our love and our fear
To give sign they are His children
One family here.

Robert Browning--Saul

Foxes rejoice--Here buried lies your foe.

Robert Bloomfield
Epitaph in an English Churchyard

All primitive peoples had a reverence for the earth. The Native American shared this ethic; the land was alive to his touch and he, its son, was brother to all creatures.

Stuart Udall--The Quiet Crisis

The Native American revered the animals he killed for food. He gathered their bones and reverently buried them, believing they would one day return to be hunted once again.

Author

Throughout the city, the talk now is of the kill, or the near kill. Some of it may even be true.

Jim Robbin
Speaking of...(A talk given in Helena, Montana, during hunting season.)

Sports in a way is like hunting, without the killing.

Author--overhead conversation

I cannot see why I should break my neck because some dog chooses to chase a nasty smell.

Arthur James Balfour--1909

Hi! Handsome hunting man,
Fire your little gun--
Bang!

Now the animal
Is dead and dumb and done,
Nevermore to peep again,
Creep again, leap again,
Eat or sleep or drink again.
Oh, what fun!

Walter DeLa Mare
The Huntsman

If there is one word in the English language I hate, it is--"game".
It seems to imply that other creatures are about for our sport.

William Holden--Actor--1972

The gentleman must realize that once he is in the saddle, he must be as
Rude as possible to anyone who crosses his path.

Douglas Southerland
The English Gentleman

The English country gentleman galloping after a fox--the unspeakable in pursuit
of the inedible.

Oscar Wilde
Woman of No Importance

Happy is the hare at morning for she cannot read the hunter's waking
thoughts.   *W. H. Auden--1960*

For man, as for flower and beast, the supreme triumph is to be most vividly,
most perfectly alive.

D. H. Lawrence--Apocalypse

The buffalos are gone
and those who saw the buffalos are gone
--are gone.

Carl Sandberg

To wear the Arctic Fox
You have to kill it!
Marianne Moore
The Arctic Fox--1959

An irate landowner during the Maine deer season posted his land: " No hunting or fishing. Survivors will be prosecuted."
Author

When a man wantonly destroys one of the works of man, we call him a vandal. When he destroys one of the works of God, we call him a sportsman and a hunter.
Joseph Wood Krutch--1961

A gun gives you the body--not the bird.
Thoreau

How strange a thing is death
Bringing to his knees,
Bringing to his antlers
The buck in the snow--
Life, looking out attentive from
The eyes of the doe.
Edna St. Vincent Millay
The Buck in the Snow

"Who saw him die?"
"I", said the fly,
"With my little eye,
I saw him die."
Anon--Who Killed Cock Robin?

"Who killed Cock Robin?"
"I", said the sparrow
With my bow and arrow
I killed Cock Robin."
Ibid

There was a little man and he had a little gun
And his bullets were made of lead, lead, lead,
He went to the brook and saw a little duck
And shot it dead, dead, dead!

Anon--There was a Little Man

There is no sport in hate
When all the rage
Is on one side.

Shelley--Lives To a Reviewer

Hurt not animals.

Triptolemus--Precepts
(Plutarch--Lives of Greek Mythology--600 B.C.)

Commenting on vanishing species, Harvard professor Edward O. Wilson said, "It's like astronomy without the stars."

A man is ethical only when all life is sacred to him--plants, animals, and his fellow man, and when he devotes himself to all life in need of help. For reverence to life is the highest appeal.

Albert Schweitzer

Impaling worms
To torture fish.

George   Coleman   the   Younger--
Commentaries

Single he was; his horns were all his helps
To guard him from a multitude of whelps

Besides a company of men were there,
If dogs should fail to strike him everywhere.

Edmund Waller--Poet--1644
(When taxed by insincerity, he replied in this rhyme.)

The Debate over Animal Rights

Massachusetts is debating a new hunting law which will outlaw leg-hold traps or other body-gripping devices which often kill people's pets when they become entrapped. Many wild animals chew off their paws in an effort to free themselves. The state has long been the conscience of human and civil rights and is now poised to become a key battleground in the calamitous fight for animal protection.

The bill will end the guaranteed convenience of hunters and increase the say of people who enjoy wildlife in their natural setting. Current law states that a majority of the board governing wildlife be composed of people "representing the fishing, hunting, and trapping interests". Should wildlife policies be directed to the benefit of these groups who hunt-fish, or trap?"

There are only 1300 registered trappers in the state, and only 2.2% of all residents over sixteen hunt and only 11% fish. This minority is overwhelmed by the 70% who enjoy wildlife in non-obtrusive ways, such as by observation and photography. Many feel it is about time we re-think the way we treat animals and the obligations we have toward them. Our present laws do not represent democracy at work.

The numbers speak for animal awareness. In 1978 the Humane Society had 78,000 members. Today there are close to half a million. PETA alone has more than 500,000, and membership in animal rights groups has grown from two million to 10 million.

Typical of the growing sentiment is Melissa Berni, a high school senior who said, "I don't think it's right to sacrifice another being for my pleasure. Things like force-feeding geese to make pate, restraining calves to make veal, removing pigs' tails and confining them too closely, transporting livestock for days without food or water just makes me sick." Berni is one of the third of teen-age girls who say they are vegetarians; and 17% of all teen-age boys have become vegetarians.

In Massachusetts both sides are girding for a fight over leg-hold traps, and the makeup of the state Fisheries and Wildlife board. Hunters insist no changes are needed and vow to stop what they consider to be a "first step to stop hunting". "This is not a good idea and not just for us but for the enhancement of wildlife in general", said Michael Yacino, executive director of the Gun Owners' Action League.

Animal advocates insist the state needs to change its thinking. "The regulated industry should not be in charge of setting the regulations", said Jerry Bertrant, president of the Massachusetts Audubon Society, "We don't want the fox in charge of the henhouse".

(Note: Hunting licenses are owned by less than 5% of the U.S. population, trapping less than 1%. *Author)*

PART II

DOGS, CATS AND OTHER ANIMALS

IN PROSE AND POETRY

DOGS

The censure of a dog is a thing no man can stand.
Max Beerbohm

Dogs display reluctance and wrath
If you try to give them a bath,
They bury bones in hideaways,
And half the time they trot sideaways
Ogden Nash

"He was always sorry when he bit someone", mother said, "but he didn't look sorry."

James Thurber--Our Dog

I can train any dog in five minutes; it's the owners that take longer.
Barbara Woodhouse

It's a terrible thing for an old lady to outlive her dogs.
Tennessee Williams

The only thing on earth a man loves more than himself is his dog.
Josh Billlings

Their tails are high, their tongues away: The true sign of huskies' contentment.

Clara Germani on Sled Dogs

He had splendid formation--broad shoulders, white hair, and erect carriage. His ensemble was a rich brown, and one was inclined to hope he would award the blue ribbon to himself

Red Smith--commenting on a dog-show judge.

On Good Friday, while meditating on the beach, I met two ladies who were very attracted attracted to my Welsh corgi and she to them. They asked her name, and when I said "Ruby", they looked at each other and burst out laughing. Both had dogs at home whose names were Ruby. The odds against this meeting were at least a million to one.

Author

A Kentucky mountaineer sitting by the fire asked his son to go outside and see if it was raining. The son, also relaxed, asked, "Can't we just send the dog outside and see if he's wet when he comes back in?
W. K. Welch

A frustrated butcher burst into a lawyer's office and asked, "If a dog steals a $5 steak off my butcher's block, is the owner liable?"

"Of course", replied the lawyer. Laughing, the butcher said, "Then give me $5. Your dog just stole it from me." The lawyer laughed and said, "Give me another $5 worth and it will cover my fee."
Southern Illinois Fable

In a rivalry, the conservative New York Post called the Sun a "Dirty Yellow Dog" Nonplussed, the Sun replied, "The attitude of this paper will be the same as any dog to a Post."
Walter Winchell

Mike Connolly told the sad tale of a man seeking to ingratiate himself into his aunt's will by being especially kind to her dogs. His ploy was successful and, when she died, she remembered him. She left him her dogs.

Beware of the silent dog, and still water.
Latin--232 B.C.

Do not keep a dog and bark yourself.
16th Century proverb

Dogs bark before they bite.
J. Heywood

Every dog is a lion at home.
Italian saying

He who would kill his dog gives out first; he is mad.
J. Ray--1687

If your old dog barks, he gives counsel.

G. Herbert--1657

When a dog is drowning, everyone gives it a drink.

Author--<u>Dialogue onDylan Thomas and Robert Benchley</u>

When your dog gnaws on a bone, companions would he none.

Latin--200 B.C.

A man, a horse, and a dog never weary of one another's company.

18th Century

Who loves me will also love my dog.

St.. Bernard of Clairvaux--13th Century

I am his highnesses' dog at Kew
Pray tell me, sir, whose dog are you?

Alexander Pope

The dog is mentioned in the bible on 17 occasions, the cat never.

Author

"Tis sweet to hear the catch-dogs'
honest bark,
Bay, deep-throated, as we
draw near home;
"Tis sweet to know there is an eye
will mark
Our coming, and look brighter when
we come.

Lord Byron--<u>Don Juan</u>

Like all kids, the little girls loved the dog...Regardless of what they say, we are going to keep it.

Richard Nixon--defending the gift of his dog, Checkers--1952

Daddy won't you buy me a bow-wow-wow,
I've got a little cat
And I'm very fond of that.
Joseph Tabrar--song

If you can't decide on a shepherd, a setter or a poodle, get all three; adopt a
mutt   *SPCA motto*

When it comes to persuading the electorate, nothing succeeds better than
having a dog. "Hell", they reason, "if he likes dogs, he can't be all bad."
Dick Gregory--1968

A dog teaches a boy perseverance, fidelity, and to turn around three times
before sitting down.
Robert Benchley--a remark at the Algonquin Round Table, 1922

Dogs' lives are too short, their only fault, really.
Agnes Sligh Turnbull

Man loves the dog because the dog is fool enough to trust man. On the other
hand, the cat obeys the Scriptures: "Put not your trust in things." The cat is like the
wise man: he trusts principle, not a man of principle.
Melvin B. Tolson Tigers, Lions and Men

He has every quality of a dog, except loyalty.
Henry Fonda from the play
The Best Man

All bachelors love dogs and would love children just as much, if they could
be taught to retrieve.
P. J. O'Rourke--1987

Are you digging on my grave--
That one true heart was left behind!
What feeling do we ever find
To equal among human kind
A dog's fidelity.
Thomas Hardy--1870

Think of the storm roaming the sky
uneasily

Like a dog looking for a place
to sleep in--
Listen to it growling.
Elizabeth Bishop--1963

I started early--took my dog--and visited the sea.
Emily Dickenson

Old mother Hubbard
Went to the cupboard
To get her poor dog a bone
But when she got there
The cupboard was bare
And so the poor dog got none.
Sarah Catherine Martin --1800

A dog knows his master, a cat does not.
Eleazar B. Zadok
Talmud--13 A.

Who breeds a wild dog in his house keeps kindness away.
Sabbath--Talmud--63 A.

Who was bitten by a dog will tremble at his bark.
Zobar--Erodus--45 A

Two dogs in a kennel snarl at each other, but when a wolf comes along, they become allies.
Sanhedrin--Talmud--105 A.

Unlike your dog, some friends are like a sundial--useless when the sun sets, for false friends, like birds, migrate when the weather turns cold
Jewish Proverb

Beware of a dog and a savior both frothing!
Hoffenstein
Pencil In the Air--1923

Recollect the Almighty, who gave the dog to be companion to our pleasures and our toils, both invested him with a nature noble and incapable of deceit.
Sir Walter Scott--The Talisman

He will hold then, when his passion shall have spent its novel force
Something better than his dog, a little dearer than his horse.
Alfred Lord Tennyson--Locksley Hall

Let your boat be light packed with only what you need--a homely home and simple pleasures, one or two friends worth the name, someone to love and someone to love you, a dog--a cat--and a pipe or two.
Jerome Klapka--3 Men in a Boat

America is a large friendly dog in a very small room. Every time it wags its tail, it knocks over a chair.
Arnold Toynbee

Where can I go
without my mount
all eager and quick?
How will I know
in thicket ahead
is danger or treasure
when Body, my good
bright dog is dead?
Mae Swenson--Question--1954

"The curious incident of the dog in the nighttime."

"But the dog did nothing in the nighttime."

"That was the curious incident", remarked Sherlock Holmes
A. Conan Doyle--Hound of the Baskervilles

There are three faithful friends--an old wife, an old dog, and ready money.
Benjamin Franklin--Poor Richard

Like a dog, he hunts in dreams.

Tennyson

I feel I have a right to resent, to object to libelous statements about my dog.

Franklin Delano Roosevelt
To critics of his dog, Fala

The quick brown fox jumps over the lazy dog.

Typing exercise using all 26 letters

Hi diddle diddle
The cat and the fiddle
The cow jumped over the moon
The little dog laughed
To see such craft
And the dish ran away with the spoon

Anon--High Diddle Diddle

Therefore to this dog will
Tenderly, not scornfully
Render praise and favor

Elizabeth Barrett Browning
To Flush, My Dog

Is it not most shameful that, in requesting favors, man should be left behind by a dog?

Philo--Trojan War

I am called a dog, because I fawn on those who give me anything, I yelp at those who refuse, and I set my teeth in rascals.

Diogenes Laertius
Greek Cynic--386 B.C.

Unmissed except by his dogs and his groom.

S. Cowper
The Progress of Error

To hear how W. Symonds do commend and look sadly--would make a dog laugh.

S. Pepys Diary--8 January 1664

So when two dogs are fighting in the street with a third dog, one of them meets with angry teeth, he bites him to the bone, and this dog smarts for what that dog has done.

Fielding--Tom Thumb the Great

The yellowest cur I ever knew
Was to the boy who loved him, true!
Unknown--The Dog

Make a dog prosperous and he will not bite you. This is the principle difference between a man and a dog.

Mark Twain

Dogs bark as they are bred and fawn as they are fed.
A. Cheales
Proverbial Folk Lore

At thieves I barked,
At lovers wagged my tail
And thus I pleased
Both Lord and Lady Frail
John Wilkes
Epitaph for Lady Frail's Dog

A waking dog doth afar off bark at the sleeping lion.
John Lyly--Endymion

I won't keep a dog and bark myself.

Jonathan Swift--Polite Conversation

The slowest barker is the surest biter.

D. Twill--Vade Mecum--1638

People who lived here long ago
Did by this stone it seems intend

To name for future times to know
The Dachshund--Geist, their little friend
Matthew Arnold--1868

He was such a dear little cock-tailed pup.
R. H. Barkham
Mr. Peters' Story

But the poor dog,
In life the firmest friend
The first to welcome
Foremost to defend.
Lord Byron
To His Newfie

Old Dog Tray's ever faithful
Grief cannot drive him away
He's gentle, he's kind,
I'll never, never find
A better friend than old dog Tray.
Stephen Collins Foster Old Dog Tray
(Foster did not write Old Dog Tray. It was written by an English poet, but Foster incorporated the poem into a most successful song which enjoyed wide popularity from 1845-1900. It was one of his first "hits".)

The curate thinks you have no soul. I know that he has none.
Sir John Lucas--The Curate Thinks

The dog is man's best friend
He has a tail at one end
Up in front he has teeth
And four legs underneath.
Ogden Nash
Introduction to Dogs

History is filled with more tales of the fidelity of dogs than of men.
Alexander Pope--Letters--1709

I love a dog of Blenheim birth,

With fine long ears and full of mirth
And sometimes, running o'er the plain
He tumbles on his nose
But quickly jumping up again,
Light lightning, on he goes.
John Ruskin--My Dog Dash--1856

Two dogs of black St. Hubert's breed
Unmatched for courage, breath and speed.
Sir Walter Scott--Lady of the Lake

The little dogs and all,
Troy, Blanche, and Sweetheart, see,
They bark at me.
Shakespeare--King Lear

And mastiff, greyhound, mongrel grim,
Hound or spaniel, brach or lym,
A bobtail type or trundle-tail
Ibid--Act III,sc.6

Mine is no narrow creed
And He who gave thee being did not frame
The mystery of life to be the sport
Of merciless man. There is a better world
For all that live and move--a better one
Where proud bipeds, who would fain confine
Infinite goodness to the little bounds
of their own charity, may envy thee.
Robert Southey
On the Death of His Favorite Spaniel--1818

We are two travelers, Roger and I
Roger's my dog--Come here you scamp!
Jump for the gentleman--mind your eye!
Over the table--look out for the lamp!
The rogue is growing a little old,
Five years we've tramped through wind and weather

And slept outdoor when nights were cold
And ate--and drank--and stayed together.
J. T. Trowbridge--The Vagabonds

The stone tells us that it covers the white Maltese dog, Fumelus' faithful companion. They called him Bull while he still lived, but now the silent paths of night possess his voice.
Tymness--400 B.C
Epitaph--Greek Anthology, Book VI

Lo, the poor Indian! Whose untutored mind
Sees God in clouds, or hears him in the wind,
His soul proud science never taught to stray
For as the solar walk or Milky Way,
Yet simple nature to his hope is giv'n
Behind the cloud-topt hill, an humbler Heav'n
He asks no angel's wing, no Seraphic fire;
But thinks, admitted to that equal sky,
His faithful dog will bear his company.
Alexander Pope--Essay on Man

When a dog runs at you, whistle for him.
Thoreau

I would rather see the portrait of a dog I know than all the allegorical paintings they can show me in the world.
Samuel Johnson--1746

Money will buy a pretty good dog but not a wag of its tail.
Josh Billings--1870

A dog (rainbow) in the morning, sailor take warning.
A dog in the night is the sailor's delight
Roper

Like a dog at the Nile (River). (Dogs run along the banks lapping furtively in fear of crocodiles.)
Adajiorum opus--1550

122

There is a dog in the well. (Something is amiss.)
J. Kelly

The dog that fetches will carry. (The talebearer will bear tales of you as well as to you.)
Scottish Proverb

He that lies down with dogs will rise with fleas.
Ibid

The bells, the iron dogs of the air
Lift up their joyful barking.
Henry Heine Kobes

If you can't run with the big dogs, make sure you stay on the porch.
Proverb

Dogs are the most gentle and trusting of all the animals.
Pindar--Greek Poet--501 B.C.

...Time was when the little toy dog was new
And the soldier was passing fair;
And that was the time our Little Boy Blue
Kissed them and put them there...
Little Boy Blue

...The gingham dog went "bow-wow-wow!"
And the Calico cat went, "Mee-ow!"
The air was littered, an hour or so,
With bits of gingham and calico...
The Duel

"I'll get you, my pretty, and your little dog, too."
The Wicked Witch to Dorothy--Wizard of Oz

Happiness is a warm puppy.

Charles Shultz--Peanuts

When a dog growls at and bites his master, it's time for a wife to pack up and go back to her mother.

Mark Twain

When all the world was young, lad,
And all the trees are green
And every goose a swan, lad,
And every lass a queen,
Then hey for boot and horse, lad,
And round the world away;
Young blood must have its course, lad
And every dog its day.

Charles Kingsley--Water Babies

There is sorrow enough in the natural way
For men and women to fill our day
When we are certain of sorrow in store
Why do we always arrange for more?
Brothers and sisters, I bid they beware
Of giving your heart to a dog to tear.

Rudyard Kipling--Power of the Dog

CATS

When you command a dog to sit up, he feels he has to. The average cat throws off pretending to be stupid, not understanding. The cat really understands you too well but sees nothing in it for him. Why sit up?

William Lyon Phelps

Cats have style and grace. Who ever heard of a dog burglar? Cats are the closest thing we will find to perfection. Owning a cat is a utilitarian pleasure and an aesthetic one. A dog is prose, a cat--poetry.

Anne Fadiman, Cat Lover

What cats appreciate in a human is not the ability to produce food, which they take for granted, but his or her entertainment value.

Geoffrey Household

We have cats like other people have mice.

James Thurber

I have just been given a charming Persian kitten...and his opinion is that I have been given to him.

Evelyn Underhill

I would never wound a cat's feelings, no matter how aggressive I am toward humans.

A. L. Rouse--Three Cornish Cats

A cat is a lion to a mouse. It is also a pigmy lion who loves mice, hates dogs, and patronizes human beings.

Oliver Hereford

Did St. Francis preach to the birds? Whatever for? Why didn't he preach to the cats? It would have been much better.

Rebecca West

Balanchine has trained his cat to perform brilliant jetes and tours l'air. He says that at last he has a body worth choreographing for.

Bernard Toper

While dining at President Coolidge's White House, the guests were unsure of their manners, so they emulated every mannerism of their host. When coffee was served, the President poured his into a saucer, then added sugar and cream. The guests did likewise. Then he leaned over and gave the saucer to his cat.

Henry Charles Suter

Whether or not it's bad luck to meet a black cat depends on if you are a man or a mouse.

Author

Nature cannot be hidden. It bursts forth in the eyes of a cat.

Irish Proverb

Hanging of a cat on Monday
For killing a mouse on Sunday.

Richard Braithwaite, Poet--1612

When I play with my cat, who knows do I make her more sport, or does she me?

Montaign--1588

A harmless necessary cat

Shakespeare

They'll take suggestion
Like a cat laps milk.

Ibid

A cat's walk--a little way and back.

W. Hazlitt--1869

A cat in gloves catches no mice.

16th Century Proverb

A cat may look at a king.

Ibid

An old cat laps as much milk as a young kitten

W. Camden--1614

Care killed a cat.

16th Century Proverb

There never was a cat or a dog drowned that could see the shore.
Italian Proverb

A blate (*shy*) cat makes a proud mouse.

Scottish Proverb

A cat would eat fish but would not wet her feet.
16th Century Proverb

A cat knows whose lips she licks

Roman--3rd Century

A cat and a dog may kiss but are none the better friends.
12th Century Proverb

It is a brave mouse that nestles in a cat's ear.
14th Century Proverb

To let the cat out of the bag. (*Secrets*)
17th Century Proverb

To turn cat in the pan. (*To change sides*)
17th Century Century

When the cat is away, the mice will play.
Anon--16th Century

Two cats and a mouse
Two wives in one house
Two dogs and a bone
Never agree in one.
J. Ray--1679

Wanton kittens make sober cats.

T. Fuller--1732

Of all creatures, there is only one which cannot be made the slave of the leash. That one is the cat. If man be crossed with the cat, it would improve the man but it would denigrate the cat.

Mark Twain--Notebook

Cat: It has been the providence of Nature to give this creatures nine lives instead of one.

Bidpat--Indian philosopher

Cruel, but composed and bland,
Dumb, inscrutable and grand,
So Tiberius might have sat
Had Tiberius been a cat.
Matthew Arnold--1860

If a dog jumps into your lap, it's because he likes you. If a cat does, it's because your lap is warmer.

A. N. Whitehead

If a fish is the movement of water embodied, given shape, then cat is the diagram and pattern of subtle air.

Doris Lessing--Particularly Cats

Cats work on the principle it never does any harm to ask for what you want.
Joseph Wood Krutch--February

Diana gives such a terrible account of your cat--such a wrecker! Alas, old animals are so much nicer. I love my cat now, but it took eight years.
Nancy Mitford

But thousands die without this or that. Die and endow a college or a cat.
Alexander Pope

A big cat, detained briefly in a poodle parlor, sharpening her claws on the velvet.
Matthew Parris, recounting Lady Thatcher detained in the House of Lords.

A cat
I keep that plays about my house

Grown fat
From eating many a miching mouse.
(Secret or hidden)
Oliver Hereford--1920

If a man might purchase a wife and love her 'til she grows as gray as a cat.
Thomas Flatman--1670--On Marriage

Here is the cat
That killed the rat,
This is the dog
That worried the cat
That killed the rat.
This is the cow
With the crumpled horn
That tossed the dog
That worried the cat
That killed the rat....
Mother Goose Rhymes

Pussy cat, Pussy cat
Where have you been?
I've been to London
To visit the Queen,
Pussy cat Pussy cat
What did you there?
I frightened a little mouse
Under her chair.
Ibid

Had the Torah not been given us, we would learn modesty from cats, honest
toil from ants, chastity from doves, and gallantry from cocks.
Edrudin--prophet--Book of Talmud

Radioactive cats have 18 half-lives.

As I was going to St. Ives
I met a man with seven wives
Each wife had seven sacks

Each sack had seven cats
Each cat had seven kits,
Kits, cats, sacks, and wives,
How many were there going to St. Ives?
Anon

The saxophones wailed like melodious cats under the moon.
Aldous Huxley--Brave New World

A man was very upset at the antics of his cat and, at a party, was telling the others all the ways he had tried to correct its bad manners. He told them he had decided to kill the cat. At this point, Dorothy Parker chimed in, "Have you tried kindness?"

Let take a cat and foster him well with milk and tender flesh, and make his couch of silk, and let him see a mouse go by, anon, he waveth milk and flesh, and all and every dainty that is in the house. Such appetite has he to eat a mouse.
G. Chaucer--Naunciples

By night all cats are grey.
Cervantes--Don Quixote

What cat's adverse to fish?
Thomas Grey

In the great open spaces
Where cats are cats
Don Marquis--Archie & Mehitabel--1912

The devil playeth oft...so does the cat with a mouse...An old cat sports not with her prey.
George Herbert

There are more ways to kill a cat than choking her with cream.
Charles Kingsley--Westward Ho

I am as vigilant as a cat to steal cream.
Shakespeare--Henry IV

When the cat winketh
Little wot the mouse what the cat thinketh.
Cats hide their claws
Thomas Fuller--Gnomologia

It would make a cat laugh.

J. R. Planch--Extravaganza

The more you rub a cat on the rump
The higher she sets her tail.
John Ray--Proverbs

He's like a cat,
Fling him which way you will, he'll light on his legs.
Ibid

She watches him as a cat watches a mouse.

Johnathan Swift--Polite Conversations

Stately, kindly, lordly friend, condescend to sit here by me.
Swinburne--To a Cat

I like little pussy, her coat is so warm,
If I don't hurt her, she'll do me no harm.
Jane Taloe

A good cat deserves a good rat. (*A bon chat, bon rat*)
A mauvais chat, mauvais rat. (*A bad cat deserves a
bad rat*)

The cat is in the parlor
The dog is in the lake,
The cow is in the hummock
What difference does it make?
Anon--Indifference

The ideal of calm exists in a sitting cat.
Jules Renard

The cat, once having sat on a hot stove lid, will not sit on a hot stove lid again, nor upon a cold stove lid.

Mark Twain

Fleas are, like the remainder of the universe, a divine mystery.

Anatole France

A kitten is so flexible that she is almost double, the hind parts are equivalent to another kitten with which the forepart plays. She does not discover that her tail belongs to her until someone steps on it.

H. D. Thoreau

A cat is out of kind when sweet cream it will not lap.

Jacob & Esau V

To see which way the cat jumps. (*On which side is he.*)
Kingsley--1863

Waddle-fat robins seek seeds in the snow,
Waddle-fat cat, hypnotizing, below,
What magic keeps hunter and hunted benign?
A double-glass patio door does just fine.
Carolynn Logan--Borders

The cat shuts its eye when it steals cream. (*Men become willfully blind to the wrongs when involved in a sin.*)
R. . Trench--Archbishop of Canterbury

The Cat, the Rat and Lovell, our Dog, rule all England under a Hog! (Richard III executed a man by the name of Collinghorne for this small rhyme about three of Richard's counselors--Lord Lovell, Sir Richard Ratcliffe, and Sir William Catesbie-- the dog, the rat, and the cat. The hog was Richard III)
Holingshed--Chronicles--1808

Like a cat on hot bricks. (*Reference to a horse stepping out in a race.*)
J. Ray--English Proverbs

A cat will be kind.
> *(Said of wicked men who will be true to their "Principles")*
> *G. Harvey--Letterbook--1500*

To make a cat's paw of...*(A person used to serve the purposes of another.)*
> *Sir Walter Scott--Journal, 1830*

The cat winked when both eyes were out. (*"I'm told for certain you were among the Philistines; no wonder the cat winked when both her eyes were out."*)
> *Johnathan Swift--1738*

Cats eat what hussies spare. *(What the good wife spares, the cat eats.)*
> *J. Clarke--1639*

Cats hide their claws. *(The tiger, when he means to prey, hides his claws.)*
> *Dekker--Ravets Almanac--1639*

The problem of cat vs bird is as old as time. If we attempt to solve it by legislation, we may be called upon to take sides as well on dog vs cat, and even birds vs worms. The State of Illinois has enough to do without trying to control feline delinquency.
> *Adlai Stevenson--Governor of Illinois, in his veto of a Bird Bill*

The trouble with a kitten is
THAT
Eventually it becomes a
CAT
> *Ogden Nash*

Yellow cat, black cat, as long as it catches mice it is a good cat.
> *Premier Deng Xiaoping-- A Saying in Sichuan Province*

Daylong the tomcat lies stretched flat
As an old rough mat,
No mouth and no eyes
Continual wars and wives
Are what have tattered his ears
And baited his tears.
> *Ted Hughes--Esther's Tomcat*

"Repent soon" thought Mehitabel, the cat, "One never knows when it will be too late." Then she reflected--"If life has a second edition, will I get a chance to correct the proofs?"

Author's thoughts on Don Marquis' Archie & Mehitabel--1912

Mehitabel continued her elocution:

> we would rather be randy, gaunt, and free
> and dine on a diet of roach and rat
> than slaves to a tame society
> ours is the zest of the alley cat
> fish heads, freedom, a frozen sprat
> dug from the gutter with digits frantic
> is better than bores and a fireside mat
> Mehitabel us for the life romantic.

Don Marquis--Archie & Mehitable--1912

A Mehitabel Romance:

but he was an elegant gent even if he was a highbrow and a regular bohemian archy him and me went aboard a canal boat one day and he got his head into a pitcher of cream and couldn't get it out and fell overboard he come up once before he drowned toujours gai kid he gurgled and then sank forever that was always his words archy toujours gai kid toujours gai I have known some swell gents in my time dearie

Ibid

I would rather be a kitten and cry mew than one of these same meter ballad singers.

Shakespeare on ballad singers

OTHER ANIMALS

Animals talk to each other. I never knew but one man who could understand them. I know because he told me himself.

Mark Twain

Bees are not as busy as we think they are. They just can't buzz any more slowly.

Frank Hubbard

The bees got their government system settled years ago, The human race is still groping.

Don Marquis

A cow drinks water by the ton
And never tastes of scotch and rum,
The dog at fifteen cashes in
Without the aid of any gin,
The cat in milk and water soaks,
And in 12 short years, it croaks,
The modest, sober, bone-dry hen
Lays eggs aplenty, then dies at ten,
The sinless live and swiftly die,
But sinful, ginful, rum-soaked men
Survive for three score and ten
And some of them, a very few
Make it clear to ninety-two.

Anon

The cow is of bovine ilk,
One end is moo, the other, milk

Ogden Nash

A fly can't bird, but a bird can fly.

Winnie the Pooh

Mohammed Ali stung like a bee
But lived like a WASP

Eamon Andrews

God, in his wisdom, made the fly
and forgot to tell us why.
Ogden Nash

Fleas are, like the remainder of the universe, a divine mystery.
Anatole France

A zoo is a place designed by animals for the study of human beings.
Oliver Hereford

The best thing about animals is they don't talk much.
Thornton Wilder--The Skin of Our Teeth

There may be flies on you and me,
But there are no flies on Jesus.
Salvation Army Song

Fog rolled in last night. It came, not on the little cat feet of Carl Sandburg's phrase, but with the authority of an elephant and with just about the same coloring.
M. Middleton, describing a London Pea Souper

Edible: Good to eat, and wholesome to digest as a worm to a toad, a toad to a snake, a snake to a pig, a pig to a man, and a man to a worm.
Ambrose Bierce--Devil's Dictionary

A fox is a wolf that sends flowers.
Ruth Weston--1955

Glories like glow-worms, afar off
            shine bright
But looked too near, have neither heat
            nor light.
John Webster--Duchess of Malfi

My heart is like a singing bird
Whose nest is in a watered shoot
My heart is like an apple tree
Whose boughs are bent with thick-set fruit.
Christina Rossetti--A Birthday

The woods decay, the woods decay and fall
The Vapours weep their burden to the ground
Man comes and tells the field and lies beneath
And after many a summer dies the swan.
Tennyson--Tithonus

The moan of doves in immemorial elms,
And murmuring of innumerable bees.
Tennyson--The Princess

There was an old hen
She had a wooden leg
And every damned morning
She laid another egg;
She was the best damned chicken
On the whole damned farm
And another little drink
Wouldn't do us any harm!
Anon--Rhyme for 19th Century drinking song

The last inn of all travelers, where we shall meet worms instead of fleas.
Sir William Davenant--The Graveman as the Master

Hold with the hare and run with the hounds.
Humphrey Robert--Complaint

How doth the little crocodile
Improve his shining tail
And pour the waters of the Nile
On every golden scale!
How cheerfully he seems to grin
How neatly spread his claws
And welcome little fishes in
With gently smiling jaws!
Lewis Carroll--Alice's Adventures

...Nevertheless it is even harder for the average ape to believe he was descended from man.

H. L. Mencken

The British upper classes cannot tolerate the notion that the stable in Bethlehem was a common farmer's stable instead of a first-rate racing one.

George Bernard Shaw--The Doctor's Dilemma

> This is the honeymoon
> of the cockroach,
> The small
> spiderless eternity of the fly.

Seamas Francis Deane

The ass who thinks himself a stag discovers his mistake when he reaches the hurdle.

Longfellow--1852

Animals, once they have gained our affection, cannot lose it. They cannot speak.

Ivan Panin

People eat animals, who eat smaller animals, smaller animals eat greens, greens eat animalculae, who eat bacilli, who in turn eat microbes which prey upon man. The cannibal takes the short cut.

Quoted in the Wall Street Journal

> The lone sheep
> is always in danger
> of the wolf.

Italian saying

There is no glory in outstripping donkeys!

Martial--Roman epigrammist--100 A.D.

They say the first inclination of an animal is to protect itself.

Diogenes Laertes--360 B.C.

Every man who has declared another an ass gets angry when the other man demonstrates the assertion was erroneous.

Friedrich Nietzsche

Bees work for man and yet they never bruise
Their master's flower, but leave it having done
As fair as ever and as fit to use
So both the flower doth stay and honey run.
George Herbert

Though lions to their enemies
They were lambs to their friends.
B. Disraeli

Little lamb who made thee?
Dost thou know who made thee?
Bid thee life and bid thee feed
By the stream and o'er the mead,
Gave thee clothing of delight
Softest clothing, woolly, bright.
William Blake

Man spurns the worm, but pauses
'Ere he wake
The slumbering venom
of the snake.
Lord Byron

Tiger, Tiger, burning bright
In the forests of the night--
What immortal hand or eye
Could frame thy fearful symmetry?
William Blake

Wee, sleekit, cow-rin, tim-rous beastie,
Oh what a panics in thy breastie!
Robert Burns--1781

Rats! They fought the dogs and killed the cats
and bit the babies in their cradles!
Robert Browning--Pied Piper of Hamelin

Feather-footed through the plashy fen, passes the questiing vole.
Evelyn Waugh--1950

I think I could turn and live with animals, they're so placid
and self-contained.
I stand and look at them long and long.
Walt Whitman--Song of Myself

The animal is very bad. When attacked it defends itself.
P. K. Theodore--1828

The Dodo never had a chance. He seems to have been invented for the sole
purpose of going extinct, and that was all he was good for.
Will Cuppy--1941

Ants are so like man as to be an embarrassment. They farm fungi, raise aphids as
livestock, launch armies into war, take prisoners for food, use chemical sprays to alarm
their enemies, capture slaves, engage in child labor, exchange information ceaselessly.
They do everything but watch TV.
Lewis Thomas--Lives of a Cell

Jim ran away from his nurse.
He slipped his hand and ran away!
He hadn't gone a yard when--bang!
With open jaws a lion sprang
And hungrily began to eat
The boy, beginning at his feet.
Hillary Belloc

Be kind and tender to the frog
And do not call him names
No animal will more repay
A treatment kind and fair
At least so lonely people say
Who keep a frog. (And by the way
They are extremely rare.)
Ibid--The Frog

Tomorrow is ours and the animals' permanent address.
e.e. cummings--(Animals)

Nobody loses all the time
my uncle Sol's farm
failed because the chickens
ate the vegetables so
my uncle Sol had a
chicken farm 'til the
skunks ate all the chickens when
(Down went uncle Sol and
started a worm farm.)
Ibid

All but blind
In his chambered hole
Gropes for worms
The four-clawed mole
Walter DeLa Mare

Happy insect, happy thou,
Dost neither age, nor winter know
Satiated with thy summer feast
Thou retir-st to endless rest.
Abraham Cowley--1860--<u>The Grasshopper</u>

I'm nobody--who are you?
How dreary to be somebody
How public like a frog--
To tell your name the live-long June
Before an admiring bog.
Emily Dickenson

Children,
Behold the chimpanzee
He sits on the ancestral tree
From which we sprang
In ages gone.
Oliver Hereford--1903

Truly, men hate the truth; they'd liefer
Meet a tiger on the road.
Therefore the poets honey their truth
with lying.

Robinson Jeffers--1923

Under the wide hearth
a nest of rattlers
they'd knot a hundred together
had wintered and were coming awake
the warming rock
flushed them out early

Robert Morgen

Camped on a tropic riverside
One day he missed his loving bride
She had, the guide informed him later
Been eaten by an alligator!
Professor Twist could but smile
"You mean", he said, "a crocodile."

Ogden Nash--The Purist

Morning and evening
Maids heard the goblins cry
One had a cat's face
One whisked a tail
One tramped at a rat's pace
One crawled like a snail
One like a wombat
Crawled obtuse and furry
One like a ratel *(badger)*
Tumbled and scurry.

Christine Geoergina Rossetti--Goblin Market

A robin redbreast in a cage
Puts all Heaven in a rage
A dog starved at his master's gate
Predicts the ruin of the state

Each outcry of the hunted hare
A fiber from the brain does tear.
William Blake--1801

Magnified 1000 times, the insects
Look farcially human;
Laugh if you will,
Bald head, stage-fairy wings, bleary eyes,
A caved-in chest, hairy mandibles
Long spindly legs.
Robert Graves--1928--<u>The Blue Fly</u>

The butterfly, a cabbage-white
(His honest idiocy of flight)
Will never, now, it is too late
Master the art of flying straight.
Ibid

The spider's touch, how exquisitively fine!
Feels at each thread, and lives along the line.
Alexander Pope--1720

I suffered for birds,
for young rabbits caught
in the mower
My grief was not excessive
For to come upon warblers
In early May
Was to forget time and death.
Theodore Roethke--1939

The minimal bacterial creepers
Wriggling through wounds
Like elvers in ponds
Their wan mouths
Kissing the warm sutures
Cleaning and caressing
Creeping and healing
Ibid

<u>The Sloth</u>
In moving slow he has no peer
You ask him something in his ear
He thinks about it for a year.
                    Ibid

The frost is on the punkin
And the fodder's in the stock
And you hear the kyouck and gobble
of a struttin' turkey cock...
                    James Whitcomb Riley--1903

Balboa lies dead somewhere
And Pizzaro's helmet
Is a spider's kingdom
                    Wilfred Townley Scott

A million butterflies
Rose up from South America
All together and few
In a gold storm toward Spain
                    Eastward,
The animal legend.
                    Ibid

The desire of the moth
for the star
                    Shelley

Hail to thee blythe spirit
Bird thou never wert
Teach me half the gladness
That thy brain must know
Such harmonious madness
From my lips would flow
As I am listening now.
                    Percy Bysshe Shelley--<u>To a Skylark</u>

My heart loves to hear the nightingales, though the songster be far away and above.
M. Ibn Ezra--AJL--164

Oh, that I might fly on Eagle's wings!
Judith Halevi--Selected Poems

I am a rainworm, buried deep
Among the oozing, slimy things,
Yet of an eagle's nest I dream
And eagle's wings.
Peret--I Am a Rainworm--1900

The codfish lays 10,000 eggs
The lowly hen lays one
The codfish never cackles
To tell you what she's done.
So we scorn the codfish
While the humble hen we prize
Which only goes to show you
It pays to advertise.
Anon

When footpads quail at the night-bird's wail,
And black dogs bay at the moon,
Then is the specters' holiday
Then is the ghosts' high noon!
Gilbert--Ruddigore, ActI

Out of the earth
I sing for them
Horse nation
I sing for them
The animals
Teton Sioux--I Sing for Them

Lo--the Turquoise Horse of Johan-ai--
There he spurneth dust of glittering grains--
How joyous his neigh.
Navaho--Song of the Horse

The black turkey gobbler, the tips of his
beautiful tail; above us the dawn
becomes yellow.
The sunbeams stream forward.
Apache--Black Turkey Chant

Even the blackest of them all, the crow
Renders good service as your man-at-arms
Crushing the beetle in its mall
And crying havoc on the slug and snail.
Henry Wadsworth Longfellow
Birds of Killingsworth

And when the jug is empty quite
I shall not mew in vain
The friendly cow, all red and white
Will fill it up again.
Oliver Hereford--The Milk Jug

Cows are my passion.

Charles Dickens--Domby & Son

Milk the cow that's near. Why pursue the one that runs away?
Theocritus--Idylls--280 B.C.

Spur not the unbroken horse.

Sir W. Sooth--The Monastery

Lord Ronald said nothing, he flung himself on his horse and rode wildly in all
directions.

Stephen Leacock--Nonsense Novels

To make a prairie it takes a clover
One bee--
If the bees are few.
Emily Dickenson--Poems, Part II

"If you were to make little fishes talk, they would sound like whales."
(Goldsmith to Dr. Johnson)--Boswell--The Life of Johnson--1773

A fly is as untamable as an hyena.

Ralph Waldo Emerson

My Aunt Catherine told me to read the life of Dr. Chalmers, a noted minister. I did not do so. Later I heard her telling Aunt Jane, who is nearly deaf: "HE WON'T READ THE LIFE OF DR. CHALMERS, but he will STAND FOR A WHOLE MORNING LISTENING TO THE CROAKING OF THE FROGS."

Henry David Thoreau

Honeyed words like bees,
Gilded and sticky, with a little sting

Eleanaor Wylie--Little Words

(The old saying "sticks and stones may break my bones, but words wil never hurt me" is incorrect. Words do sting and linger on all our lives. Author)

Fish say they have their stream and pond;
But is there anything beyond?

Rupert Brooke--The Hill--1915

At least,
Love your eyes that can see,
Your mind that can
Hear the music
The thunder of the wings
Love the wild swan.

Robinson Jeffers--Love the Wild Swan--1935

Another armored animal--scale
lapping scale with spruce cone regularity until
they
form the uninterrupted central
tail row.

Marianne Moore--The Pangolin--1941

Camels are snobbish
And sheep, unintelligent;
water buffalos, neurasthenic

even murderous,
Reindeer seem over-serious
Ibid--The Arctic Ox

The lazy geese, like a snow cloud
Dripping their snow on the green grass,
Tricking and stopping, sleepy and proud
Who cried in goose--alas
John Crow Ransom--Bells

When hairs stand on end and a shiver runs down your back, and your skin crawls when one writes or reads a true poem it is because the true poem is necessarily an invocation of the White Goddess, or Love, the Mother of All Living, the ancient power of fright and lust--the female spider or the queen bee whose embrace is death.
Robert Graves--The White Goddess--1948

It was the best place to be, thought Wilbur, this warm delicious cellar, with the garrulous geese, the changing seasons, the heat of the sun, the passage of swallows, the nearness of rats, the sameness of sheep, the love of spiders, the smell of manure, and the glory of everything.
E. B. White--Charlotte's Web

I meant what I said
And I said what I meant
An elephant's faithful
One hundred percent.
Theodore Seuss Geisel--Dr. Seuss

A slow drip over stones
Toads brooding in wells
I shook the softening
Chalk of my bones
Saying,
Snail, snail glisten me forward
Bird, soft-sigh me home
Worm, be with me
This is my hard time--
Theodore Roethke--The Lost Son

...and honored among foxes and pheasants
by the
gay house
Under the new-made clouds and happy as the
heart was long.
In the sun barn over and over
I ran my heedless ways.

Dylan Thomas--Fern Hill

He has an angry wren-like vigilance
A greyhound's gentle tautness--

Walter Lord--Poetic Images

Hear the lonesome whippoorwill
He sounds too blue to fly
The midnight train is whining low
I'm so lonesome I could cry.

Hank Williams--song
The Lonesome Whippoorwill

Sacred cows make the tastiest hamburger.

Abby Hoffmann--(an aside attributed to him)

When you were a tadpole
and I was a fish
In the Paleozoic Time,
My heart was rife with the joy of life
And I loved you even then.

Langdon Smith--Evolution--1895

The rat is no concistent tenant,
He pays no rent--
He cannot harm
A foe so reticent.

Emily Dickenson

Too late repents the rat
When caught by the cat.

John Florio--Second Frutesu--1587

150

Ride a cock-horse to Banbury Cross
To see a fine lady on a white horse
Rings on her fingers, bells on her toes
And she shall have music where she goes.
Nursery Rhyme
(The big cross at Banbury was destroyed in 1601)

Worms lurk in all; yet proest they to worms
Who from Mundingo sail.
James Grainger--The Sugar Cane
Lewis and Lee in The Stuffed Owl refer to this poem as the worst in the language.
"They" refers to slaves.)

Do you realize, Fred, what a rare thing a friend is? When you think of all the terrible
people there are in this world, animals are much better than people. God, I love animals!
That's what I like about you, Fred. You're so fond of animals.
Dorothy Parker--Just a Little One

I heard a little bird say so.
Johathan Swift--Letter to Stella
("A little bird said so" is very old. It may come from a passage in the Bible: "for a
little bird shall carry the voice"--Ecclesiastes 10:30)

He is a fool that lets slip a bird in the hand for a bird in the bush.
Plutarch--200 A.D.

Birds of a feather will gather together.
George Whetstone
(This is a proverb which has been found in the earliest annals of recorded history.)

He thought he saw an elephant
That practiced on a fife:
He looked again and found it was
A letter from his wife.
"At length I realized", he said,
"The bitterness of life."
Lewis Carroll--Sylvia & Bruno V

Little Bo Peep has
Lost her sheep
And doesn't know where to find them
Leave them alone and they'll come home
Wagging their tails behind them.
Nursery Rhyme
(The Elizabethan game of Bo-peep played for babies, was what we call Peek-a-Boo)

If you enjoyed the Rainbow Bridge, you may wish to pass along a copy to a friend. To do so, send along $17.95 (We will pay the $3.00 postage) by check or money order to:

Running Tide Press
c/o Paul Dahm
Box 302
Oceanside, OR 97134

Please include your name, address and number of copies

Also, if you have had a similar experience or have a friend who has had one, send it along to the above address. Running Tide Press will pay $50-$100 for each story which becomes a part of Rainbow Bridge--Book II.